THE 8051 FAMILY OF MICROCONTROLLERS

RICHARD H. BARNETT, PE, PhD
Purdue University

Prentice Hall
Englewood Cliffs, New Jersey   Columbus, Ohio

Library of Congress Cataloging-in-Publication Data

Barnett, Richard H.
    The 8051 family of microcontrollers / Richard H. Barnett.
        p.   cm.
    Includes index.
    ISBN 0-02-306281-9
    1. Intel 8051 (Computer) 2. Digital control systems. 3. Embedded
computer systems.   I. Title.
QA76.8.I27B37   1995
004.165—dc20

94-25810
CIP

Editor: Dave Garza
Production Editor: Mary Harlan
Cover Designer: Gryphon III
Cover photo: Comstock
Production Buyer: Pamela D. Bennett
Editorial/production supervision and interior design: Spectrum Publisher Services

This book was set in Times Roman by Bi-Comp, Inc., and was printed and bound by Book Press, Inc., a Quebecor America Book Group Company. The cover was printed by Phoenix Color Corp.

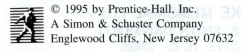

Prentice-Hall International (UK) Limited, *London*
Prentice-Hall of Australia Pty. Limited, *Sydney*
Prentice-Hall of Canada, Inc., *Toronto*
Prentice-Hall Hispanoamericana, S. A., *Mexico*
Prentice-Hall of India Private Limited, *New Delhi*
Prentice-Hall of Japan, Inc., *Tokyo*
Simon & Schuster Asia Pte. Ltd., *Singapore*
Editora Prentice-Hall do Brasil, Ltda., *Rio de Janeiro*

For Rosemary,
without her support,
encouragement, and gentle nudges
this book would not exist.

PREFACE

The aim of this text is to present sufficient information so that the reader will understand the 8051 family of microcontrollers and be able to develop a project using these devices. The material is presented in a handbook format so that any topic can stand on its own. In other words, studying the entire book will prepare the reader to complete a design using an embedded controller. Later, when working on designs, the text will function as a handbook in which details and program examples can be quickly located.

The languages used are assembly language and C language. Assembly-language programming is covered in some detail, but it is expected that the reader will learn C elsewhere. Examples are presented in both forms to provide the greatest range of examples for the reader. Some projects virtually require the use of assembly language, while most others lend themselves to the greater convenience of a high-level language such as C. Where it might be helpful, the author has tried to point out the relative merits of each language for the specific example. The program examples have been assembled/compiled with the assembler and compiler produced by the Franklin Co.[1]

Embedded controllers are designed to control electronic and mechanical equipment. This book includes many real-world examples in which the microcontroller is interfaced to real devices using standard interface techniques. Included are interface methods such as power drivers, analog-to-digital conversion, digital-to-analog conversion, and others. Some familiarity with these devices may assist the reader in understanding the examples, but every effort has been made to ensure that the examples can stand on their own.

The hardware examples in this book have either been built and tested or are slight modifications of working systems. The software examples have been tested with real hardware. In other words, every effort has been made to minimize the error content. The author cannot, however, guarantee that errors do not exist, nor can he accept any responsibility should you choose to use a circuit or program presented herein.

It is strongly suggested that the *8-Bit Embedded Controllers Handbook* and the *8051 Applications Manual* be obtained from Intel[2] and the *Signetics Microcontroller User's Guide* be obtained from Signetics.[3] These three books, although similar, tend to complement one another and provide a complete reference to the microcontroller family.

Normally, both companies are happy to provide the books free for educational purposes. Contact the companies or a local sales representative to check on availability.

ACKNOWLEDGMENTS

I wish to thank the following colleagues for their constructive comments in reviewing the manuscript: Tony Alumkal, Austin Community College; David Delker, Kansas State University; Omer Farook, Purdue University–Calumet; Subramaniam Ganesan, Oakland University; David Jones, Lenoir Community College; Todd Morton, Western Washington University; Chandra Sekhar, Purdue University–Calumet; James Stewart, DeVry Institute of Technology–Woodbridge, NY; Neal Widmer, Purdue University.

REFERENCES

1. Franklin Software, Inc., 888 Saratoga Avenue #2, San Jose, CA 95129.
2. *8-Bit Embedded Controllers Handbook* and *8051 Applications Manual,* Intel Corporation, 3065 Bowers Avenue, Santa Clara, CA 95051. Note: These handbooks change titles from year to year. In requesting these books, some variation in the title may be found.
3. *Signetics Microcontroller User's Guide,* Signetics Corporation, 811 E. Arques Avenue, P.O. Box 3409, Sunnyvale, CA 94088.

CONTENTS

INTRODUCTION

I-1   OVERVIEW OF MICROCONTROLLERS

The 8051 family of embedded controllers is descended from the very first microprocessor, Intel's 4004. The 4004 was a 4-bit general-purpose microprocessor incorporated into products as a way to add ''intelligent'' control to the products. The 4004 was, at the very least, a success. The success led designers to request more processing power, to which Intel responded with the 8008, then the 8080, and then the 8085, all of which were 8-bit general-purpose processors. Other manufacturers also responded, including Motorola with the 6800 and ZILOG with the Z80. The race was on to develop bigger and more powerful microprocessors. As time passed, the 8086 family and the 68000 family of processors emerged and are still growing today.

The limited processing power of the 4-bit general-purpose processor had pushed clever applications engineers to learn how to stretch the 4-bit processor to the very limit of its ability as an embedded device controller. When the 4-bit machines had been stretched to the limit of their ability, the designers asked for bigger machines, but it had become evident that a 4-bit processor could do a very fine job as an intelligent controller for many products. Today, microwave ovens, TVs, and many other products still contain 4-bit microcontrollers.

The 8-bit processors that emerged following on the heels of the 4004 were also general-purpose processors. Eight-bit general-purpose processors used as controllers did indeed provide more power for bigger jobs, but they also brought a larger price tag to embedded product control. Not only were the processors more expensive, the cost of peripheral devices and circuit boards increased as well. The cost of assembling the controller with the myriad of wiring required to assemble a complete microcomputer including CPU, memories, and I/O peripherals increased alarmingly. Many manufacturers retained the 4-bit designs simply because moving up to 8-bit general-purpose processors for use as controllers was too expensive for the resulting increase in processing power.

It was apparent that more highly integrated processors were needed that would provide more processing power but require less assembly time.

The result was the development of families of microcontrollers, devices that include all the system components, in addition to the processor, in a single IC package. These single-chip microcontrollers are designed to be embedded directly into commercial products at reduced cost. Most varieties of microprocessors have now been spun off into families of embedded microcontrollers. Embedded microcontrollers are, in fact, single-chip microcomputers.

The "family tree" of microprocessors is shown in Figure I–1. It is evident that only the 4-bit general-purpose processor has fallen by the wayside. The other types of microprocessors have all spawned microcontroller descendants following their development as general-purpose processors.

The microcontrollers that appeared are more than simply reduced-assembly-time microprocessors; they are a new breed of processor, optimized for control tasks rather than for "byte crunching" or mathematical manipulations. The 8051 family of microcontrollers is one of the most widely applied and copied family of microcontrollers. It has been licensed to several companies to either second source or to improve and upgrade while maintaining language and functional compatibility with the original Intel product.

The microcontroller systems shown in Figures I–2 through I–4 provide examples of the changes produced by embedded controllers. The three designs shown offer very similar functions. Each provides two or more parallel ports for control, and each can measure up to eight analog signals. The first design (Figure I–2) is based on an Intel 8085 8-bit general-purpose processor and includes separate ROM and RAM in addition to an Intel 8255 parallel port chip and an analog-to-digital converter. Also included are the necessary demultiplexor latch, address decoder, and buses. The 8085-based system is perhaps a bit large for a simple control application, but when compared to the functionally equivalent systems that follow, it clearly demonstrates the changes occasioned by the evolution of microcontrollers.

The designs shown in Figures I–3 and I–4 are based on microcontrollers of the 8051 family. The design shown in Figure I–3 uses a standard 8051 microcontroller. The microcontroller contains the ROM, RAM, and I/O for the system. In addition to the microcontroller, an external analog-to-digital converter allows analog measurement of up to eight inputs. This design shows a striking reduction in parts, reducing assembly time and cost drastically when compared to 8085-based design.

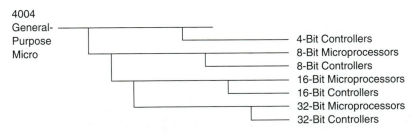

FIGURE I–1   Microprocessor family tree.

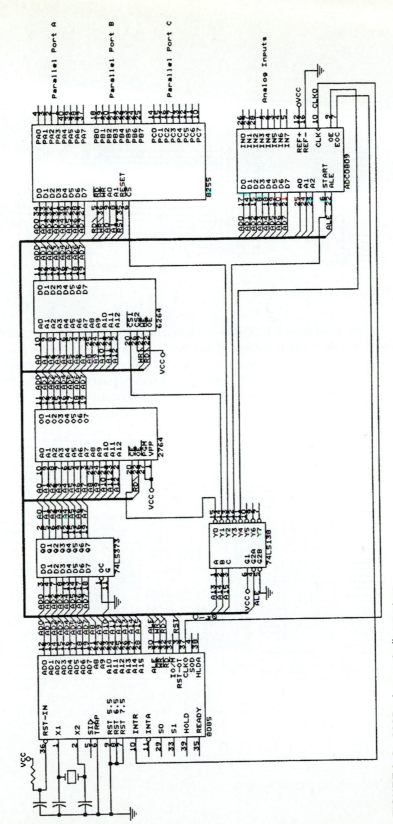

FIGURE I-2 8085 microcontroller system.

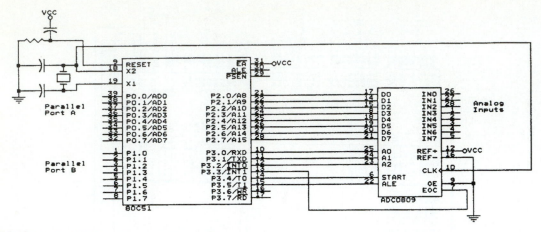

FIGURE I-3   80C51 microcontroller system.

The third design, Figure I–4, is based on a Signetics 83C552 embedded controller, which is an upgraded version of the 8051. This controller provides eight channels of analog-to-digital conversion and a number of other features not found in the basic 8051 family parts. This system is the most compact, even though it provides the most features. It is presented only as a means to provide comparison.

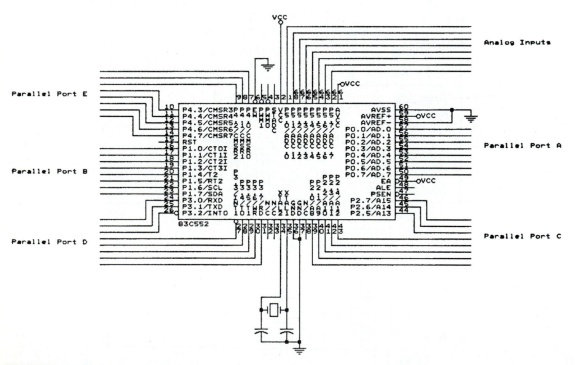

FIGURE I-4   83C552 microcontroller system.

TABLE I–1 Major parts cost

Item	8085	8031	83C552
EPROM	$ 4.95		
RAM	6.75		
Latch	.24		
Decoder	.65		
Port	2.95		
A/D	4.54	$4.54	
Processor	1.95	4.51	$8.50
Total	$22.03	$9.05	$8.50

Although the three designs will do essentially the same job and provide nearly identical functions, the latter two designs lack the data storage of the 8085 system, and the 8255 parallel port is capable of more sophisticated data transfer methods than the 8051 ports. However, the latter designs include two or three timers and serial communication, which the 8085 system cannot provide without the addition of further peripheral devices. The 83C552 system also has 10-bit resolution (resolution and ADC devices are discussed in Chapter 5) from its analog inputs. The major parts (ICs) cost analysis shows a serious cost difference and would, by itself, justify the use of the simpler circuits (see Table I–1). Although not detailed here, it is fairly clear that the cost of producing the three designs would also greatly favor the microcontrollers.

I–2 PROJECT DEVELOPMENT AND DESCENDANT PROCESSORS

Project development centered around the 8051 family of microcontrollers is a relatively painless process. One of the many descendants of the basic 8051 family will fit the needs of almost any project. They are almost 100% compatible to the 8051 core, and all the information in the book is germane since it centers on the common features of the family. In any case, where a specific descendant is known to vary from the norm, it is pointed out.

I–3 DEVELOPMENT AIDS

The author has developed an exceptionally complete developmental monitor program with an associated downloader. Educational institutions are welcome to this software by requesting the same from:

Richard H. Barnett, PE, PhD
Department of Electrical Engineering Technology
1415 Knoy Hall of Technology
Purdue University
West Lafayette, IN 47905-1415

The monitor may also be made available to individuals or to commercial interests. Contact the author at the address above for details.

THE 8051 FAMILY OF MICROCONTROLLERS

CHAPTER 1

Microcomputer Fundamentals

OVERVIEW

This chapter presents an overview of microcomputer architecture, and provides the necessary background for the balance of the book. After reading this chapter, the reader will be knowledgeable about the structure of microcomputers and their buses and control lines, and with the flow of data on the buses, which allows the microcomputer to operate.

1–1   BASIC MICROCOMPUTER ARCHITECTURE

All computers are composed of three major sections: the central processing unit (CPU), the memory, and the input/output (I/O) section. A microcomputer is made up of these same blocks, except they are physically smaller (as compared to the early computers that occupied whole rooms). A microcomputer consists of a microprocessor (the CPU equivalent), memory, and I/O. Although all microcomputers are composed of the same three basic elements, differences in the functioning of these elements distinguish one type of microcomputer from another. Figure 1–1 shows the three parts of the microcomputer and provides the basis for the following discussion.

Microprocessor

The purpose of the microprocessor block is to control the microcomputer and to carry out the instructions in the program. It provides the ''intelligence'' or decision-making capability for the system. The microprocessor reads the instructions from memory and then carries out, or executes, those instructions. Executing the instructions may involve transferring data to or from the memory or I/O sections.

The microprocessor block is also composed of three parts: the arithmetic logic unit (ALU), the timing and control (T/C) section, and the register section. The ALU is used

1

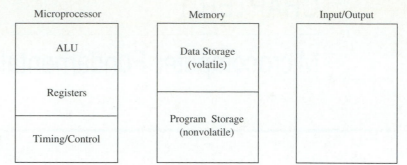

FIGURE 1–1   Basic parts of a microcomputer.

to complete all of the mathematical and logical operations necessary. In other words, it is actually the portion of the microprocessor responsible for decision making that provides the intelligence of the microprocessor. The ALU serves as the "brain," but it needs data in order to complete its mission.

The T/C section of the microprocessor is responsible for seeing that the necessary data are provided to the ALU and delivered from the ALU to other parts of the microcomputer. It is responsible for controlling the flow of data through the microcomputer system and providing all necessary timing signals to synchronize data flow.

The register section of the microprocessor is the only section of the microprocessor that is controlled directly by the programmer. It consists of a set of registers (byte-size latches) that are used by the programmer to hold and manipulate data. The register section is similar to a scratch pad in that it is used to hold all the intermediate steps as problems are solved.

Memory

The second section of a microcomputer is the memory section, which has two purposes. The first purpose is to store the program. The program consists of instructions that tell the microcomputer how to carry out its tasks. The microcomputer is ready to run its program as soon as power is applied. Consequently, the program must be stored permanently in the microcomputer, in a permanent or nonvolatile type of memory. Data stored in nonvolatile memory is not affected when the power is removed from the microcomputer.

The second purpose of the memory section is to provide an area for the microcomputer to write and store the data that it needs as it operates. This area of memory is usually volatile or nonpermanent memory. The contents of this type of memory are lost when power is removed.

Input/Output

The third and final section of the microcomputer is the I/O section. This section includes various methods to move data into or out of the microcomputer system. Examples of I/O are the serial lines to a video screen (usually referred to as a CRT, which stands for cathode-ray tube) and a keyboard, the lines that control relays or motors in an embedded microcomputer application, the devices to measure or supply analog voltages, keypads, liquid-crystal displays (LCDs), and so forth. Any device that converts binary data from inside the microcomputer into another form for use by nonmicroprocessor devices or that converts data into a form for use by the microcomputer is considered to be I/O.

1-2 MICROCOMPUTER BUS STRUCTURE

The three basic blocks of the microcomputer are interconnected so that they can exchange data and work together to accomplish the tasks given to the microcomputer. The interconnections are called **buses.** Each bus consists of a number of wires or connection paths, usually connected in a parallel fashion between devices. There are three buses used in microcomputer systems: the data bus, the address bus, and the T/C bus.

The data bus is a bidirectional bus that carries data from the microprocessor to the memory, to the I/O sections, or to the microprocessor from either of the other two sections. The memory and I/O sections do not normally exchange data directly.

The address bus is a unidirectional bus that specifies the specific device or location to be the source or destination for the data flow from or to the microprocessor. The microprocessor drives the address information onto the data bus prior to each exchange of data with the memory or I/O sections.

The T/C bus is usually a unidirectional bus that provides the signals to control the direction and timing of data flowing on the data bus. In other words, the T/C bus controls whether the data is flowing into or out of the microprocessor and determines the instant at which the data is placed onto the bus. Figure 1–2 shows the basic parts of the microcomputer system (as shown in Figure 1–1) with the buses added.

Each I/O device has one or more addresses assigned to it, and each memory cell (typically an 8-bit or byte-size cell) has its own **address.** The microprocessor uses these addresses to exchange data with the memory and I/O sections via the buses. The sequence

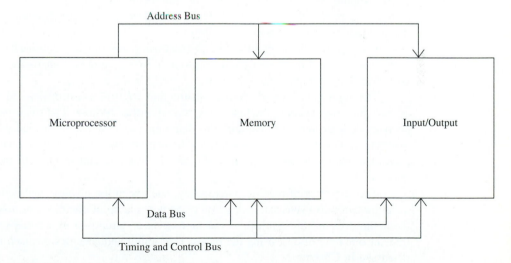

FIGURE 1–2 Microcomputer system.

of bus events to exchange data are, in simplified form:

1. The microprocessor (specifically, the T/C section) asserts the address of the device that will be either the source or destination for the data exchange onto the address bus.
2. The T/C section then asserts control signals that determine whether data is to be *read by* or *written by* the microprocessor. Data *read by* the microprocessor flows from the memory or I/O sections to the microprocessor. In this case, the memory or I/O section is the source of the data and the microprocessor is the destination for the data. Data *written by* the microprocessor flows to the memory or I/O sections. In this instance, the microprocessor is the source of the data and the memory or I/O sections are the destination for the data.
3. The data is then asserted onto the data bus by the source device, and the destination device reads the data from the data bus.

The previous sequence allows the microprocessor to read or write data using the buses. The buses allow the parts of the microcomputer to exchange data as required by the program to complete a task.

1–3   PROGRAM FLOW AND CONTROL

A microcomputer follows the instructions stored in its program memory to complete its assigned task(s). These instructions amount to a ''to do'' list of steps the microcomputer goes through to do its job.

The instructions are stored one after the other in the program or code area of the memory section. The microcomputer begins to execute the program immediately following a reset. A reset is usually forced by the hardware upon the application of power to the microcomputer system. After the reset, the microcomputer begins executing the program stored at a predetermined address. Most microprocessors begin execution at program memory address 0x0000 following a reset.

In executing the program, the microprocessor reads and performs each of the instructions in sequence. In a correctly written program, completing each instruction in sequence will eventually complete the entire task.

The microprocessor reads each instruction by first asserting its address onto the address bus, then reading the instruction stored at that address. The microprocessor then decodes or interprets the instruction to determine what steps are needed to execute the instruction. The microprocessor executes the instruction (which may involve transferring more data via the buses), then reads the next instruction, and so on until the program is concluded.

The sequence of reading, interpreting, and executing a single instruction is known as an **instruction cycle.** An instruction cycle is made up of one or more **machine cycles** (sometimes called bus cycles). A machine cycle is composed of the steps necessary to transfer one byte of data using the buses. The timing and specifics of machine cycles are discussed in Chapter 2.

1–4   SUMMARY

This chapter presents the basic system architecture of the microcomputer. The microprocessor, memory, and I/O sections of a microcomputer intercommunicate via the buses of the system to execute the program of the microcomputer. The program is executed by the microcomputer by reading in the instructions stored in program memory and carrying out those instructions one after the other to complete its task.

1–5   EXERCISES

1. Explain the difference between a microcomputer and a microprocessor.
2. Name the three parts of a microcomputer, and describe the purpose of each.
3. Name the three parts of a microprocessor, and describe the purpose of each.
4. What are the three buses of a microcomputer system? What are their purposes?
5. Which bus controls the direction of data flow?
6. What is an address? How does the address relate to memory or I/O devices?
7. What is a program?
8. Describe how a program is executed by a microcomputer. Denote which buses are used during each step and what information is being transferred by the buses as each step occurs.
9. Describe machine and instruction cycles.
10. How do machine and instruction cycles relate to Exercise 8?

CHAPTER 2

8051 Embedded Controller Hardware

OVERVIEW

Chapter 2 presents the hardware and interconnections associated with 8051 microcontrollers, including descriptions of the physical structure of the buses, the nature of memory systems, and the timing and flow of signals on the buses. After reading Chapter 2, the reader will be able to design the basic hardware portion of an 8051-based controller project.

2–1   8051 FAMILY EXTERNAL SYSTEM ARCHITECTURE

The 8051 family is a collection of embedded controllers with the same core features, including an 8-bit CPU (comprised of an ALU, T/C section, and register set), two counter timer peripherals, and the parallel and serial I/Os. The variety of additional features available in the 8051 family is shown in Table 2–1.

Table 2–1 shows the 8051 family as produced by INTEL. Other manufacturers, such as Signetics, have upgraded the family to include additional features. These upgrades extend the capabilities of the microcontroller family while maintaining language and architectural compatibility.

The core features are arranged into the CPU, the memory, and the I/O sections in the same manner as in other computer systems. The major difference of the 8051 family is that most or all of these sections are contained in a single integrated circuit (IC). Even though some of the sections are integral to the IC, communication between sections takes place via the usual buses. In some 8051 family members, all the sections are not internal to the IC. The 8031, for instance, does not contain internal program memory (see Table 2–1). In these instances the 8051 family controllers use devices connected to external buses in exactly the same manner as do most processors. An 8031 may have external code memory, or additional external data memory, or additional peripheral devices such as serial or parallel ports added by connecting them to the buses of the microcontroller.

TABLE 2–1   8051 family

ROM Version	ROMLESS Version	EPROM Version	ROM Bytes	RAM Bytes	I/O Ports	Timers	Power Control	Inter- rupts	Notes
8051AH	8031AH	8751H	4K	128	4	2	No	5	
8052AH	8032AH	8752H	8K	256	4	3	No	6	1
80C51BH	80C31AH	87C51	4K	128	4	2	Yes	5	
83C51FA	80C51FA	87C51A	8K	256	4	3	Yes	14	2
83C51FB	80C51FB	87C51FB	16K	256	4	3	Yes	14	2
83C452	80C452	87C452	8K	256	5	2	Yes	9	

Notes: 1. Some versions include a BASIC language interpreter.
2. Also includes a programmable counter array.

The distinction between code and data memory is an important feature of the 8051 microcontrollers. The 8051 departs from the traditional microprocessor in that it has separate memory address spaces for data and for program code. Further, data spaces exist both internal to the microcontroller IC and external to the microcontroller. The program space is 64K bytes of program code, which may be external or internal (up to 4K bytes). The internal data space is 128 bytes of read/write memory internal to the device, and the external data space is an additional 64K bytes outside the device. General-purpose microprocessors have only a single memory space, which must be shared between code and data.

The program code space options are denoted by the columns headed Read Only Memory (ROM), ROMLESS, and Erasable Programmable Read Only Memory (EPROM) versions in Table 2–1. The versions shown under ROM contain a mask-programmable ROM and are usually reserved for mass-produced devices where the program code is fixed and unlikely to change. Those parts listed as ROMLESS require an external memory device to hold the program code. The EPROM versions contain code memory comprised of EPROM and are usually used in the developmental stages of a project.

External connections to the 8051 microcontroller are shown in Figure 2–1, which displays the pinout diagram for the 8051 microcontroller. The pins are grouped where applicable. The four I/O ports are shown along with their alternate functions. In a basic

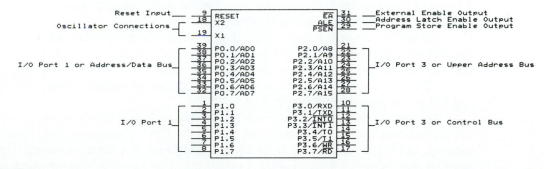

FIGURE 2–1   8051 pinout.

8051 system the four ports would function as 8-bit parallel ports. When external peripherals or memory are needed, ports 0, 2, and 3 assume their alternate roles as bus interfaces. Port 0 becomes the 8-bit multiplexed address/data bus, port 2 becomes the upper byte of the address bus, and some of the pins of port 3 become control lines such as $\overline{\text{RD}}$ (read) or $\overline{\text{WR}}$ (write).

The Reset input must be held high briefly at power-up to allow the microcontroller to initialize itself and begin execution at location 0000h. The oscillator lines are for the on-board system clock oscillator.

Other control lines include the address latch enable (ALE), the program store enable (PSEN), and the external access (EA). The ALE is used to demultiplex the address/data bus. The $\overline{\text{PSEN}}$ is used to access program memory. The $\overline{\text{EA}}$ is used to force the microcontroller to look in external code space for its instructions.

Figures 2–2, 2–3, and 2–4 illustrate the hardware used to assemble a complete 8051-based controller system. Details of the various sections of the system will be covered in subsequent chapters. The examples are functionally identical: They each show an analog data-gathering system with keypad to set up data recording parameters, an LCD display for operator feedback, eight channels of analog data inputs, and a serial port to transfer the data to a personal computer.

The 8031 data collection system (Figure 2–2) shows an 80C31 operating with external program memory and external data storage memory. In terms of the basic microcomputer architecture discussed in Chapter 1, this circuit uses the 8031 as the CPU, an EPROM (U1) as nonvolatile program memory, and a RAM (U4) as volatile data memory. The LCD (U6), the keypad (KP1), the serial communication (the 8031 and U10), and the ADC (U5) make up the I/O section.

The 80C31 contains no internal program storage memory, and thus requires an EPROM (U1) to hold the operating program for the processor. The $\overline{\text{EA}}$ pin must be set low to force the controller to access external code space for its program. A RAM (U4) is included to increase the data storage capacity of the system. The RAM, LCD, and analog-to-digital (A/D) converter are memory mapped (they occupy external data space just as external data memory would, and are addressed as external data memory) into the system through the use of a 74HC138 (U7) address decoder.

Serial communication (RS 232) is provided by the serial port internal to the 80C31 and the MAXIM MAX 233 circuit used to convert the voltage levels from TTL to RS 232 and from RS 232 to TTL. A 74HC76 (U9A) flip-flop lowers the clock frequency by a factor of 2 to provide an appropriate clock for the A/D converter, and the 74HC02 NOR gates are used to provide proper timing of the access signals.

The 80C51 system in Figure 2–3 is identical except that the program code is stored in ROM internal to the processor and the EA/Vpp pin (U2, pin 31) is pulled up to enable code access from the internal ROM. In terms of the basic system described in Chapter 1, the CPU and program storage are both internal to the 80C51 and the volatile memory and I/O are the same as in Figure 2–2.

The 80C51 minimum data collection system (Figure 2–4) is similar in function but has limited data storage capacity. In this design the CPU, program storage, volatile memory, and I/O are all internal to the 80C51. This design is a radical departure from previous designs in that it does not use a typical microprocessor bus structure. Lack of

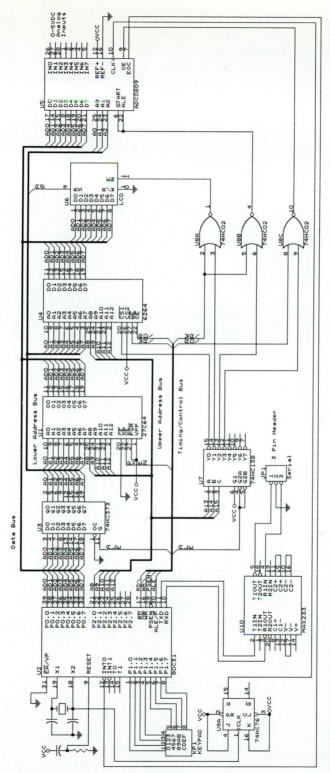

FIGURE 2–2 8031 data collection system.

9

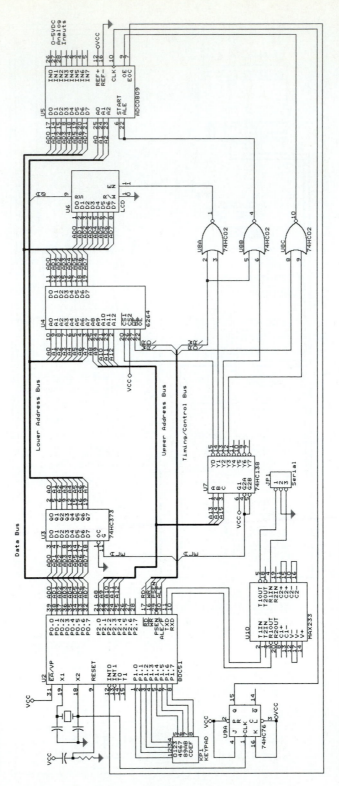

FIGURE 2-3 8051 data collection system.

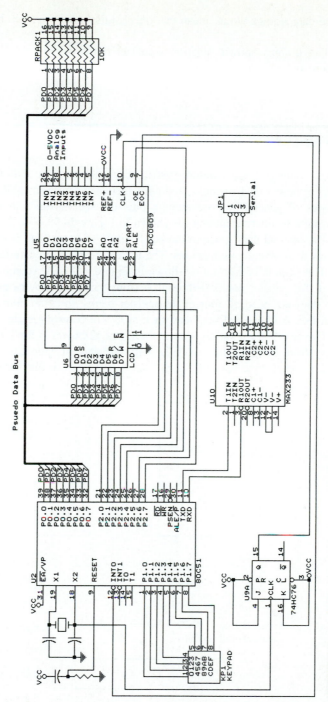

FIGURE 2–4 8051 minimum data collection system.

external data storage would mean that only a little more than 100 bytes of data could be stored.

The designs shown function similarly but differ in memory usage and design approach. In order to clarify the differences it is necessary to understand the memory organization of the 8051 family of controllers.

2-2   8051 FAMILY MEMORY ORGANIZATION

The 8051 family uses a memory system composed of three major spaces: internal data memory, external data memory, and code memory. The internal data memory is usually 128 bytes of general-purpose storage plus the special-function registers (SFRs). The organization of internal memory is shown in Figure 2–5.

The internal data space in the 8051 family of controllers is divided into two major divisions with several subdivisions. The lower 128 bytes are available in all 8051 family parts. This area is broken up as shown in Figure 2–5. The lower 32 (20 hex) bytes are reserved for register banks 0 through 3 (four banks of 8 bytes each). If your program design does not need all four of the register banks, then the unused bytes are freed for general use. A high-level language such as C will control register bank allocation.

The next highest subdivision of the lower 128 bytes is the bit-addressable memory. Memory from 0x20 through 0x2F is both byte and bit addressable. That is, there is an address for each byte (0x20 through 0x2F) *and* for each bit (0x00 through 0x7F). The

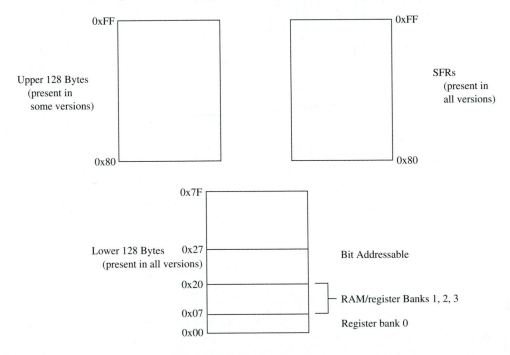

FIGURE 2–5 Internal memory organization.

TABLE 2–2 Special-function registers

Register	Address	Register Name
A (or ACC)*	0xE0	Accumulator
B*	0xF0	B register
DPL	0x82	Data pointer low byte
DPH	0x83	Data pointer high byte
IE*	0xA8	Interrupt enable
IP	0xB8	Interrupt priority
SCON*	0x98	Serial control
SBUF	0x99	Serial data buffer
PSW*	0xD0	Program status word
PCON	0x87	Power control
TCON*	0x88	Timer/counter control
TMOD	0x89	Timer/counter mode
TH0	0x8C	Timer/counter 0 high byte
TL0	0x8A	Timer/counter 0 low byte
TH1	0x8D	Timer/counter 1 high byte
TL1	0x8B	Timer/counter 1 low byte
P0*	0x80	Port 0
P1*	0x90	Port 1
P2*	0xA0	Port 2
P3*	0xB0	Port 3
Available in 8052 family parts only:		
T2CON*	0xC8	Timer/counter 2 Control
TH2	0xCD	Timer/counter 2 high byte
TL2	0xCC	Timer/counter 2 low byte
RCAP2H	0xCB	T/C 2 capture high byte
RCAP2L	0xCA	T/C 2 capture low byte

*Bit-addressable register.

lowest bit of byte 0x20 is addressed as bit 0x00, the next highest bit in byte 0x20 is addressed as bit 0x01, and so on up to the highest bit of byte 0x2F, which is addressed as bit 0x7F. The bit-addressable memory is a very efficient way to implement flags (single bits used to indicate the state of the program) and suchlike without using up whole bytes of memory. The bits are usually referred to by their bit address or by a combination of the byte and bit number within the byte (i.e., the lowest bit of byte 0x20 would be referred to as bit 0x00 or as bit 0x20.0, the next would be 0x01 or 0x20.1, the highest bit of byte 0x24 would be bit 0x27 or bit 0x24.7, etc., and the highest bit-addressable bit would be bit 0x7F or bit 0x2F.7). The bit-addressable bytes are also available for general usage.

The balance of the lower 128 bytes is free for use by the programmer. For further details, see Chapter 3, Figure 3–1.

The upper 128 bytes of internal memory contain the SFRs. These may be accessed only by using direct addressing techniques (i.e., the memory cell is referred to directly by its address). The SFRs and their addresses are listed in Table 2–2. Although the SFRs do not use all the available addresses, the unused addresses are *not* available for storage purposes. Some of the SFRs are bit addressable; their bits may be manipulated or tested directly. The SFRs are described in subsequent chapters as they are used.

Some versions of the 8051 family (see Figure 2–1) have an additional 128 bytes of internal data memory. This memory occupies the same address range as the SFRs but is accessed when indirect addressing techniques (i.e., referring to a register that, in turn, contains the address of the memory cell) are used. Addressing techniques are discussed in Chapter 3.

The second major division of data memory is external data memory. External data memory consists of up to 64K bytes of storage with addresses of 0x0000 to 0xFFFF. The external data memory is accessed only through indirect addressing using the data pointer (DPTR) to hold the address of the external memory cell. Since it holds an address, the DPTR must be a 16-bit register. DPTR is actually made up of two 8-bit registers, Data Pointer Low (DPL) and Data Pointer High (DPH). The timing and control (T/C) bus signals that control the external data memory are active low read ($\overline{RD}$) and active low write ($\overline{WR}$) along with the address lines. These are described more fully in Section 2–3.

The last major division of memory is code memory. Code memory is a 64K-byte space with addresses 0x0000 through 0xFFFF. Since these are the same addresses as for external data space, some method must exist to differentiate between the two spaces. The differentiator is the control line in the T/C bus that is used to access each space. As mentioned earlier, the control lines used to access external data space are $\overline{RD}$ and $\overline{WR}$. The control line used to access code space is Program Store Enable ($\overline{PSEN}$). Thus $\overline{PSEN}$ is the code space equivalent to $\overline{RD}$ for external data space. There is no code space equivalent to $\overline{WR}$, since there are no instructions that permit writing to code space. Normally, code space is accessed directly by the processor to retrieve instructions, but it can also be read indirectly by the programmer through the use of the DPTR.

A majority of the 8051 family controllers contain some internal program storage memory. The use of internal and external code storage space is relatively automatic. While the processor is accessing memory addresses below its maximum internal code memory limit, it looks at internal code memory for the byte of data. When the processor attempts to access memory above its maximum internal code memory limit, it looks in external code memory. In controllers that have no internal code space, or if the designer wishes to ignore the internal code memory and use only external code memory, the External Access ($\overline{EA}$) control line must be pulled to logic low. With $\overline{EA}$ low, the controller accesses external code space for all of its program instructions. With $\overline{EA}$ pulled high, the processor automatically accesses internal or external space depending on the address.

Both external data and external code memory are used in the system shown in Figure 2–2. The EPROM contains the program code (note that $\overline{EA}$ is low, forcing the processor to look in external code space for the code) and is enabled via $\overline{PSEN}$. The RAM chip is mapped into external data space and is accessed via $\overline{RD}$ and $\overline{WR}$.

In the system in Figure 2–3, the program code is stored in the internal ROM. Hence EA is pulled high to allow the processor to use the internal code storage up to the limit of its capacity. The RAM in this system is still mapped into the external data space.

The last design, shown in Figure 2–4, uses neither the external code storage space nor the external data storage space. The result is that only the internal data storage space is available for data. This design does not use typical bus architecture, but instead uses

TABLE 2–3 Alternate port 3 functions

Port 3 Bit	Bit Name	Alternate Function
0	RxD	Receive serial I/O data
1	TxD	Transmit serial I/O data
2	INT0	Input for interrupt 0
3	INT1	Input for interrupt 1
4	T0	Input for timer 0
5	T1	Input for timer 1
6	WR	Control line for external data space
7	RD	Control line for external data space

the I/O ports to implement a ''pseudo-bus'' for data flow manually, using I/O techniques. More details about usual bus architecture are given in the next section.

2–3   BUS ARCHITECTURE

The internal I/O of the 8051 consists of four 8-bit parallel ports, P0 through P3 (these are covered in detail in Section 2–5). A number of situations can, however, reduce the available parallel I/O. For example, Port 3 has alternate functions assigned to all of its bits; see Table 2–3. The use of the alternate functions is discussed later, but it is important to understand now that using a bit for its alternate function precludes its use for I/O.

Using external code or data memory also reduces parallel I/O. Such use disables ports 0 and 2, since they become the address/data and upper address buses, respectively (Figure 2–6).

Figure 2–6 shows the bus structure when accessing external memory spaces. The structure includes a 16-bit address bus, an 8-bit data bus, and at least 4 bits for control. The lower byte of the address bus is time multiplexed with the data on the same bus.

FIGURE 2–6 Bus architecture.

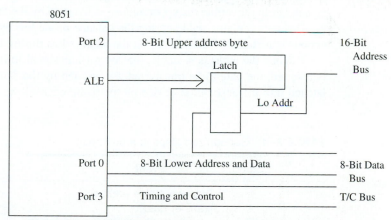

The Address Latch Enable (ALE) signal is used to demultiplex (or capture) the lower byte of the address (see Section 2–4 for more details). In this way the entire 16-bit address remains stable while the data bus is being used for data transfer.

The T/C bus is used to control the flow of data within the system. The $\overline{\text{RD}}$ and $\overline{\text{WR}}$ lines control data flow from and to the external data space, respectively. $\overline{\text{PSEN}}$ controls the flow of data from the external code space. These lines are discussed in detail in Section 2–2.

This architecture makes no allowance for a separate I/O space (for other peripherals, etc.) in addition to the memory spaces. Consequently, any external peripherals included in the system must be memory mapped, that is, treated as memory using addresses in the external data space or the external code space (read-only devices in the code space). Although this reduces the amount of memory that can be added to an 8051 system, it really causes no problems since very few controller designs ever need the entire available space. For examples of memory-mapped peripherals, see Figure 2–2 or 2–3. Figure 2–4 shows a system in which the external memory spaces are not used and hence ports 0 and 2 can function as parallel I/O.

2–4   BUS CONTROL SIGNALS TIMING

An understanding of the timing and flow of signals on the buses is important to understanding the operation of the 8051 controller. The generalized sequence of events is shown in Table 2–4. The more detailed steps are shown in Table 2–5. Figure 2–7 shows the same information in the form of waveforms.

The waveforms shown in Figure 2–7 depict the relationship of the control signals to the flow of data on the 8051 buses. The three possible external bus cycles are code read, data read, and data write. Only one of the three can occur at any point in time.

All of the bus cycles include the address-latching portion of the cycle to demultiplex the address/data bus. At the beginning of the cycle the lower address byte is asserted on port 0 (the data bus). This byte is latched into the latch on the falling edge of the ALE signal. During this time the upper address is asserted by the 8051 on the address bus (port 2). This byte remains stable during the balance of the bus cycle. The result of these two actions is a stable 16-bit address on the address bus during the entire bus cycle.

When the address is stable, the control line signal to be used ($\overline{\text{PSEN}}$, $\overline{\text{RD}}$, or $\overline{\text{WR}}$) is asserted, the data to be transferred are asserted by the source device, and the data are latched into the destination device on the rising edge of the control line signal.

TABLE 2–4   Generalized steps in a bus cycle

Step	Event
1	Output a stable address
2	Transfer data

TABLE 2–5 Generalized and detailed steps in a bus cycle

Step	Event
1	Output a stable address
	A Output the high byte of the address on the address bus
	B Raise the ALE line
	C Output the low byte of the address on the data bus (port 0)
	D Lower the ALE to latch the low address byte
2	Transfer data
	For a code space read:
	A Lower PSEN
	B Read data supplied by code memory on data bus (port 0)
	C Raise PSEN
	For an external data space read:
	A Lower RD
	B Read data from external data memory on data bus (port 0)
	C Raise RD
	For an external data space write:
	A Output data to data bus (port 0)
	B Lower WR
	C Raise WR

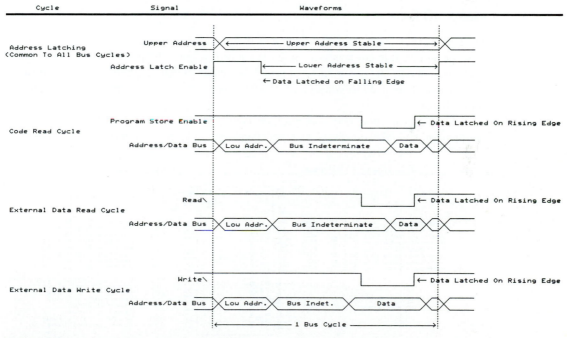

FIGURE 2–7 Waveforms of 8031 bus cycles.

The waveforms show that while the ALE is high, the address bus (both bytes) is in transition. During the transition time it is possible to get false triggering from the memory address decoder (refer to Figures 2–2 and 2–3). In order to prevent such false triggering, the ALE signal is usually applied to one or more of the memory decoder enables (the G2 enables in this example). The result is that the memory decoder is disabled while ALE is high (during the address transition period), thus preventing false triggering.

2–5   I/O SYSTEMS

The 8051 family members each have four 8-bit internal parallel ports and one internal serial port for I/O. As discussed earlier, the limitations imposed by the number of pins on the package make it necessary for most port pins to have an alternate function as well (Figure 2–8).

Unfortunately, a port pin serving in its alternate function cannot also be used for normal I/O. As shown in Figure 2–8, an 8051 with external memory (using ports 0 and 2 as buses, and port 3, bits 6 and 7, for RD/WR control lines), a serial port (port 3, bits 0 and 1), and interrupts and timers (port 3, bits 2 through 5) has only one port (port 1) available for I/O. Bits of port 3 that are not used for an alternate function may be used for I/O, but bits of port 2 that are not used for addressing may *not* be used for I/O. Designs that require more I/O than is available on the 8051 must add external I/O.

Internal I/O Ports

The four parallel ports are all configured as bidirectional ports and may be used for either input or output. It is not necessary to initialize or configure the ports for input or output, because each port bit (except those of port 0) is weakly pulled up internally when emitting a 1 and actively pulled low when emitting a 0. Figure 2–9 shows an approximate schematic for each port.

Only an *effective* port configuration is shown in Figure 2–9; that is, details are omitted for the sake of clarity and understanding. The configuration shown does not

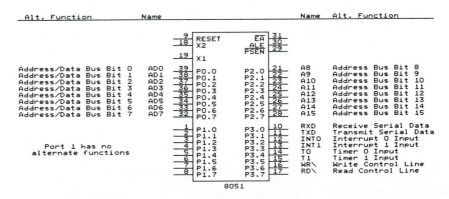

FIGURE 2–8 8051 port pins' alternate names and functions.

Port 0

Ports 1,2,3

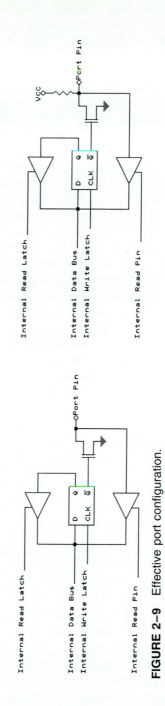

Internal Read Latch

Internal Data Bus
Internal Write Latch

Internal Read Pin

Internal Read Latch

Internal Data Bus
Internal Write Latch

Internal Read Pin

VCC

Port Pin

Port Pin

FIGURE 2–9 Effective port configuration.

19

indicate, for instance, the additional circuitry necessary for reading the alternate input functions or for using the ports as address/data buses. Although there is no pull-up on port 0 when it is functioning as I/O, the port is actively pulled up when it is used as the address/data bus.

As an example, consider the case when the microcontroller attempts to read from bit 0 of port 1. Regardless of the logic level actually being input to the bit, if the port latch bit is holding the Field Effect Transistor (FET) on (outputting a logic zero), the micro can only read the state of the bit as a 0. If, however, the FET is off, the external logic level can easily overcome the weak pull-up, and the logic level corresponding to the external signal will be read correctly.

The key to understanding internal I/O operation is that either the processor port latch or the external circuitry can pull the port bit low. Hence it is necessary to assure that a logic 1 is written to the latch of any bit that is to be used as input. In this way the input port pin's state is controlled by the external circuitry.

Figures 2–2, 2–3, and 2–4 show the use of port 1 for internal I/O, in this case to scan a 16-key keypad. As connected, the 8051 would drive bits 0, 1, 2, and 3 with the scanning signals to the columns of the keypad and read the keypad rows on bits 4, 5, 6, and 7. (See Chapter 5 for details of keypad scanning). This example illustrates that input and output functions may be mixed on the internal ports.

Figures 2–2, 2–3, and 2–4 also illustrate the use of alternate functions on port 3. The end-of-conversion signal is tied to interrupt 0 (port 3, bit 2), and serial I/O is implemented through port 3, bits 0 and 1 (RxD and TxD). Figure 2–4 shows the use of ports 0 and 2 as internal I/O. This example creates a pseudo-data bus where P0 is used to read data from the A/D converter and to write data to the LCD. The necessary pseudo "control" signals are asserted by using port 2 as internal I/O under the programmer's control.

A similar way to expand input ports is to use buffers. Figure 2–10 shows the use of buffers to expand the discrete inputs. The system shown uses one 8-bit port (port 3) for data and one 8-bit port for control (port 1). These 16 bits allow inputs of 64 bits of data from the ports labeled A through H. The processor asserts a low to the enable of one of the tri-state buffers, which allows its data to pass through to port 1 to be read by the processor. The only penalty to this type of I/O expansion is speed: Only one 8-bit set can be read at any given instant, and it requires several instructions to read any 8-bit data byte. A similar scheme could be used for outputs with octal latches instead of tri-state buffers, or a mix of buffers and latches would allow expanding both input and output.

External I/O

Additional I/O beyond what is available on the processor may also be added as memory-mapped devices. The additional I/O devices may be additional parallel I/O or other peripherals such as LCDs, real-time clocks, and so on. INTEL's 8255 parallel peripheral interface (a parallel port device) or 8253/4 counter/timer devices are occasionally added to expand the I/O capabilities of the 8051. Examples of added I/O devices are shown in Figures 2–2 and 2–3, in which the LCD and A/D converter are memory mapped into external data space.

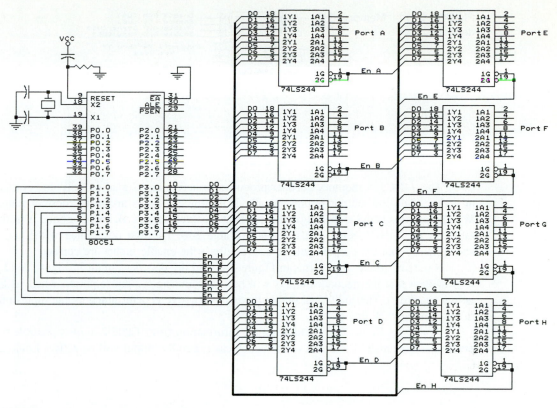

FIGURE 2–10 Expanded internal I/O.

2–6   MEMORY SPACE MAPPING AND DECODING

Each memory cell and each register of an external memory-mapped device must have a unique address. Having more than one device respond to a given address on the address bus will cause bus conflicts (more than one device attempting to drive data onto the bus at one time) and result in system crashes. The designer of the address decoding system is responsible for ensuring that no conflicts occur.

The memory system usually includes more than a single memory or I/O device. Devices are assigned separate addresses in order to prevent conflicts. The system must include a method to activate the various devices when their assigned addresses appear on the bus. The usual method is to use a memory decoder to break the memory space into parts or sections. These sections then are assigned or connected to a given device, which further decodes the addresses as it needs them.

The examples shown in Figures 2–2 and 2–3 use external memory and I/O devices all of which reside at separate addresses within the external data space. A memory decoder (U7 in the examples) is used to assign memory section addresses to each device. The memory decoder from the two figures is shown in Figure 2–11.

FIGURE 2–11 Memory decoder.

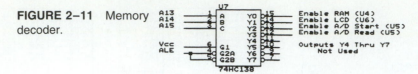

The 74HC138 memory decoder produces an active low signal on only one output at a time. The low output is present only if the three enables are in the correct state. Which output is active depends on the inputs at the decoder's A, B, and C inputs. A truth table for the 74HC138 decoder is given in Table 2–6. The first three lines of the table show clearly that the outputs will be active only if the enable inputs are correct.

Referring to the waveforms in Figure 2–7 and the decoder circuit in Figure 2–11, it is evident that the decoder outputs will be active during the entire period when ALE is low (inactive). The individual output that will be active is determined by the inputs on decoder pins A, B, and C.

Analyzing Figure 2–11 and using the information from Table 2–6, it is possible to determine the range of addresses over which each decoder output will be active. Look at

TABLE 2–6 74HC138 decoder truth table

Inputs						Outputs							
$\overline{G2A}$	$\overline{G2B}$	G_1	A_0	A_1	A_2	$\overline{Y}_0$	$\overline{Y}_1$	$\overline{Y}_2$	$\overline{Y}_3$	$\overline{Y}_4$	$\overline{Y}_5$	$\overline{Y}_6$	$\overline{Y}_7$
H	X	X	X	X	X	H	H	H	H	H	H	H	H
X	H	X	X	X	X	H	H	H	H	H	H	H	H
X	X	L	X	X	X	H	H	H	H	H	H	H	H
L	L	H	L	L	L	L	H	H	H	H	H	H	H
L	L	H	H	L	L	H	L	H	H	H	H	H	H
L	L	H	L	H	L	H	H	L	H	H	H	H	H
L	L	H	H	H	L	H	H	H	L	H	H	H	H
L	L	H	L	L	H	H	H	H	H	L	H	H	H
L	L	H	H	L	H	H	H	H	H	H	L	H	H
L	L	H	L	H	H	H	H	H	H	H	H	L	H
L	L	H	H	H	H	H	H	H	H	H	H	H	L

H = high voltage level.
L = low voltage level.
X = don't care.

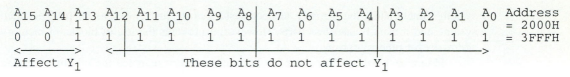

A_{15}	A_{14}	A_{13}	A_{12}	A_{11}	A_{10}	A_9	A_8	A_7	A_6	A_5	A_4	A_3	A_2	A_1	A_0	Address
0	0	1	0	0	0	0	0	0	0	0	0	0	0	0	0	= 2000H
0	0	1	1	1	1	1	1	1	1	1	1	1	1	1	1	= 3FFFH

<----->   <--->
Affect Y_1 These bits do not affect Y_1

FIGURE 2–12 Address summary chart.

the LCD output in Figure 2–11 as an example. The LCD enable is tied to decoder output Y_1. Table 2–6 shows that activating Y_1 requires levels of 1, 0, and 0, respectively, on the A, B, and C inputs. Since the A, B, and C inputs are getting their data from A_{13}, A_{14}, and A_{15}, respectively, it follows that A_{13}, A_{14}, and A_{15} must be 1, 0, and 0, respectively, to activate the LCD. Therefore, any address containing 001 in the A_{15}, A_{14}, and A_{13} (note the reversal of order to put the Most Significant Bit [MSB] at the left-most position) positions will activate Y_1.

The address summary chart in Figure 2–12 shows all the bits of the address bus. The addresses are determined by holding the determinant bits (A15, A14, A13) constant while allowing the other bits (those that do not affect Y_1) to vary from their lowest to their highest value. The range of addresses produced are those that will cause Y_1 to activate and therefore are the range of addresses that will activate the LCD. Most I/O devices, including the LCD and A/D converter shown, do not need the entire range of addresses available on any one decoder output. The actual use of addresses will be considered in later chapters with each I/O device, as will the need for the NOR gate (U8) in Figures 2–2 and 2–3.

Memory decoding may be either full or partial. Full memory decoding is shown in Figure 2–2 for the 6264 memory (U4). In this case the full range of unique addresses is used. The tell-tale feature of a fully decoded circuit is that all of the available address lines are used in the decoding. A partially decoded circuit, however, occurs when one or more address lines is not used in the decoding process. An example is the LCD (U6) in Figure 2–2. Address lines A13, A14, and A15 are used to decode the section of memory addresses assigned to the LCD. Address line A0 is used directly with the LCD; lines A1 through A12 are not a part of the decoding scheme. The result is a partially decoded

FIGURE 2–13 Memory map for Figure 2–2.

External Code Space

0FFFFH

08000H

06000H

04000H

02000H

00000H

| U3 |
| Program ROM |

External Data Space

| Read A/D |
| Start A/D |
| LCD Display |
| U4 Data RAM |

system. Functionally, the partially decoded system works just as well as the fully decoded system, and it usually uses less parts. However, it prevents the use of blocks of memory addresses for other purposes.

Figure 2–13 shows the complete external memory map for the circuit of Figure 2–2. The addresses shown are all those that will affect the device, and the solid lines denote areas of memory actually used in this project.

2–7   SUMMARY

This chapter presents the hardware aspects of 8031 microcontroller systems. The family of microcontrollers is described, showing that some devices have internal program memory and some do not. The 8031 may be used as an independent device or as an element of a microcomputer system. Memory decoding is used to differentiate among various memory devices. Using a knowledge of memory decoders, it is possible to analyze or design the memory system address assignments.

2–8   EXERCISES

1. Use Table 2–1 to select a member of the 8031 family for a design that requires 4K of ROM, power control, and 97 bytes of internal RAM.
2. Name the alternate functions for each of the pins of port 3.
3. Describe the SFR section of the 8051 family. Name 10 SFRs and describe their use.
4. Determine the bit addresses for the following:
   (a) Bit 0x56 is bit 0x____.____.
   (b) Bit 0x4F is bit 0x____.____.
   (c) Bit 0x26.6 is bit 0x____.
   (d) Bit 0x2B.2 is bit 0x____.
5. Describe each of the steps of the machine cycle necessary to transfer data from the memory to the microprocessor.
6. Why may two internal port pins be tied together even though one is attempting to output a logic 0 while the other is outputting a logic 1? What logic level will be seen on the two pins?
7. What is the purpose of a memory decoder?
8. Draw a simple block diagram of a project consisting of an 8051 with one external ROM for program storage and two external data storage devices (RAM). Include all necessary connections for the latch, control lines, and memory decoder.
9. Develop a memory map for the circuit shown in Figure 2–14. Determine whether each device is fully or partially decoded.
10. Design a memory system (figure out how to connect a 74HC138 decoder) to divide the external data space into 16 4K blocks. Draw out the decoder schematic and show all connections to the buses.

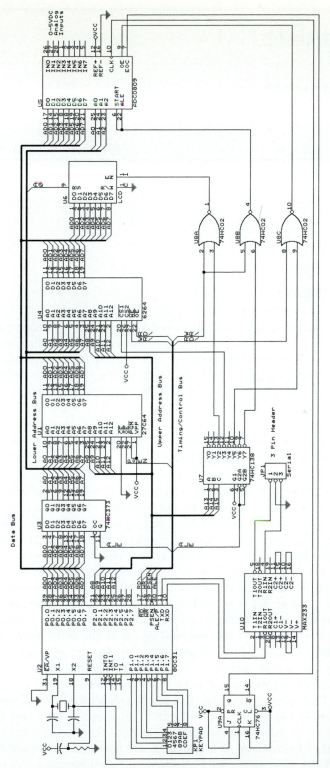

FIGURE 2–14 Practice system.

CHAPTER 3

Software

OVERVIEW

Software and software-related issues associated with embedded controllers are the major topics of this chapter. Assembly-language programming, 8051 family internal architecture, program development, and the 8051 family instruction set are stressed. After completing this chapter, the reader will be prepared to develop simple assembly-language programs for use with 8051 family microcontrollers.

3-1   8051 FAMILY SOFTWARE OPTIONS

A wide variety of programming language options exist for the 8051 family of microcontrollers. They may be programmed using assembly language or any of several high-level languages. Examples of high-level languages available for the 8051 family include C, BASIC, Forth, and PL/M. In order to understand the options, it is important to understand machine language, assembly language, and high-level language.

Machine language consists of numbers that the microcontroller can interpret as commands and data to tell it how to perform its task. An example of machine language would the sequence of bytes 0x02, 0x00, 0x30 stored in program space. These numbers are interpreted by the microcontroller as a jump (0x02, the operational code or **opcode**) to a location (0x0030, the **operand** or data). The instructions used by the 8051 may consist of 1, 2, or 3 bytes, depending on the amount of data needed by the instruction. All of the various languages available to the programmer must be reduced to machine code for the microcontroller to be able to use them.

Each of the instructions that can be executed by the microcontroller has a unique opcode (first number) associated with it. Since opcodes are very difficult for humans to use, each opcode is represented by a written, English-like version called an **assembly-language instruction.** The instruction for the sequence shown above would be: JMP 0x0030. In other words, the instruction set for a microcontroller consists of instructions and are the lowest-level commands available to the programmer. Several examples of opcodes and instructions are:

Opcode	Instruction	Comment
0x02	ljmp	Long jump
0xe2	movx	Transfer data externally
0x24	add	Add values

These examples show clearly the difference between the machine language and the instruction set. The instruction set is for human use, and machine language is for the machine.

The instruction set for the 8051 family is a rich set of instructions including features that are designed to be convenient for control-oriented applications. Examples of these conveniences include Boolean or bit-oriented operators for all internal ports and numerous special-function registers, bit-addressable RAM for use as flags, and a fairly open register usage format. Each of these terms will become clear in succeeding sections.

Assembly-language programs consist of instructions from the 8051 instruction set and data bytes as required by the individual instructions. Assembly language allows total control over execution timing and memory usage. This generally means that the program code can be made more compact and that execution timing can be controlled exactly. When memory is limited or timing is critical, it may be mandatory to use assembly language. The major disadvantage of assembly language is that the programmer must attend to every detail associated with the program, including memory allocation for code and data, use of registers, and control of variable storage.

Higher-level languages, those a distance "above" the machine-language level, relieve the programmer from the details associated with assembly-language programming. These languages consist of more readable (English language-like) statements that are finally compiled or translated into machine language for the microcontroller. Memory allocation, variable security, stack utilization, and many other details are handled by the language compiler. The disadvantage, of course, is that the programmer loses control of these details. Usually the machine code resulting from a high-level language program will be significantly larger and slower than the code from an assembly-language program that accomplishes the same task.

The choice of programming language depends on the project. Writing a successful program in any language, however, requires a thorough understanding of the processor's internal architecture.

3-2 8051 FAMILY ARCHITECTURE

The CPU in the 8051 family is an 8-bit processor that, like most CPUs, is composed of three sections: an arithmetic logic unit (ALU), a timing and control (T/C) section, and a set of registers (8-bit storage locations within the microcontroller) generally available to the programmer.

The ALU is responsible for mathematically changing data bytes. It handles addition, subtraction, multiplication, division, and logical operations such as logical ANDing or ORing of data. The ALU section is internal to the microcontroller CPU and is not under the programmer's direct control.

The T/C section is responsible for synchronizing the flow of data into and out of the CPU. It coordinates the movement of data on the buses both inside and outside of the microcontroller. The T/C section generates the $\overline{\text{PSEN}}$, $\overline{\text{RD}}$, and $\overline{\text{WR}}$ signals discussed in Chapter 2.

The only section of the CPU that is directly controllable by the programmer is the register section. Registers are byte-wide latches used to hold and manipulate data. The registers of most microprocessors include an accumulator, a data pointer register, and other general-purpose registers. The register section of the 8051 family is actually made up of two register groups, the special-function registers (SFRs) and the register banks.

The SFRs are really the crux of the 8051 architecture. Every normal processor register and special function (except the register banks) is an SFR in the 8051 family. In

TABLE 3–1 Special-function registers

Register	Address	Register Name	Reset
A (or ACC)*	0xE0	Accumulator	0x00
B*	0xF0	B register	0x00
DPL	0x82	Data pointer low byte	0x00
DPH	0x83	Data pointer high byte	0x00
IE*	0xA8	Interrupt enable	0x00
IP	0xB8	Interrupt priority	0x00
SCON*	0x98	Serial control	0x00
SBUF	0x99	Serial data buffer	????
PSW*	0xD0	Program status word	0x00
PCON	0x87	Power control	0x00
TCON*	0x88	Timer/counter control	0x00
TMOD	0x89	Timer/counter mode	0x00
TH0	0x8C	Timer/counter 0 high byte	0x00
TL0	0x8A	Timer/counter 0 low byte	0x00
TH1	0x8D	Timer/counter 1 high byte	0x00
TL1	0x8B	Timer/counter 1 low byte	0x00
P0*	0x80	Port 0	0xff
P1*	0x90	Port 1	0xff
P2*	0xA0	Port 2	0xff
P3*	0xB0	Port 3	0xff
Available in 8052 family parts only:			
T2CON*	0xC8	Timer/counter 2 control	0x00
TH2	0xCD	Timer/counter 2 high byte	0x00
TL2	0xCC	Timer/counter 2 low byte	0x00
RCAP2H	0xCB	T/C 2 capture high byte	0x00
RCAP2L	0xCA	T/C 2 capture low byte	0x00

* Bit-addressable register.

other words, the accumulator (A) is an SFR, the peripherals are controlled via SFRs, the data pointer is an SFR, the ports are SFRs, and so forth. For the most part, all SFRs can function much like accumulators, making programming fairly simple and convenient. Control of all internal features is accomplished via one or more SFRs. The data pointer (DPTR), for instance, is a pair of SFRs [data pointer low (DPL) and data pointer high (DPH)] that form the pointer to all external memory.

An important characteristic of SFRs is their reset value. Upon power-up or reset of the 8051, certain SFRs are forced to contain specific values. These are important to disable features that could cause erratic or unpredictable operation of the microcontroller or its peripherals. The reset or default values of the SFRs are shown in Table 3–1. The need for these values will become apparent as the SFRs are discussed.

As shown in Table 3–1, each SFR has its own address. The SFRs are all located in the upper 128 bytes (above 0x7F) in internal RAM space. They may be written or read using direct addressing (covered in more detail later in this chapter) techniques. Although the SFRs do not use all of the available addresses in the upper 128 bytes of memory, the unused addresses are not available for data storage or any other use: The memory cells at these addresses simply do not exist.

The second section of registers are the general-purpose registers. These registers are called R0 through R7 and are grouped into four banks of 8 bytes each. The registers of each bank provide handy temporary storage of intermediate values. Further use of the register banks will become evident as the languages are discussed in upcoming sections.

These three sections, the ALU, T/C, and registers, make up the CPU of the 8051 family. The CPU is only a portion of the microcontroller that is contained within the 8051 microcontroller IC package. RAM storage area and a variety of peripherals are also included in the 8051. The RAM is covered as a part of this chapter, and the peripherals are discussed in Chapter 4.

3–3   MEMORY ARCHITECTURE

The internal memory organization of the 8051 family of microcontrollers reflect their intended use. Microcontrollers need to be convenient to program and use. Consequently, they contain a significant internal RAM area for the programmer's use. The complete memory maps for internal and external memory are shown in Figures 3–1 and 3–2, respectively.

The internal data RAM of the 8051 is composed of four distinct segments. The lower 32 (00 through 0x1F) bytes make up the four register banks of 8 bytes each. These register banks are simply groups of 8 bytes that may be used for general-purpose storage and that, for convenience, may be referred to by their names—R0 through R7. The active (currently used) bank is determined by the contents of register bits RS0 and RS1 in the processor status word (PSW) SFR. Only one register bank may be active at a time.

The next higher segment of internal RAM is composed of the 16 bit-addressable bytes (0x20 through 0x2F). These locations may be used as normal 8-bit storage registers; or the individual bits may be set, cleared, or tested using Boolean instructions. The individual bits are most often useful as flags.

FIGURE 3–1 Internal memory organization.

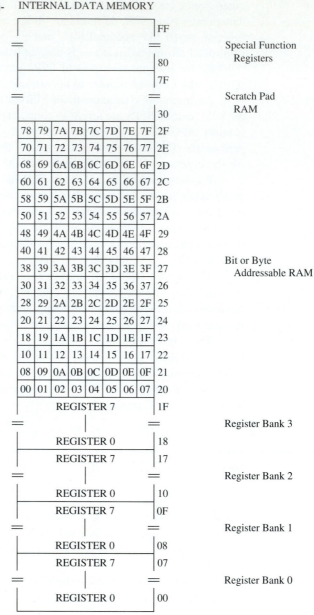

INTERNAL DATA MEMORY

The balance of the internal RAM (0x30 through 0x7F) is available for general-purpose byte-size storage. The area above 0x7F (0x80 through 0xFF) is dedicated to SFRs.

The lower internal RAM (below 0x80) may be addressed directly (by specific address) or indirectly using R0 or R1 as a pointer. Indirect addressing consists of using a register to contain the address of the memory location to be used. This register then

FIGURE 3–2 External memory organization.

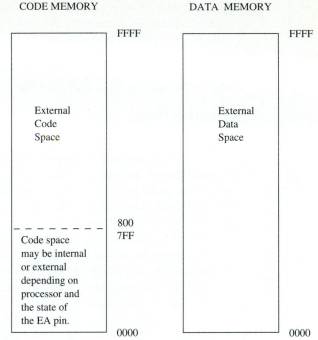

CODE MEMORY

External
Code
Space

FFFF

800
7FF

Code space
may be internal
or external
depending on
processor and
the state of
the EA pin.

0000

DATA MEMORY

External
Data
Space

FFFF

0000

can be referred to as an indirect pointer to the memory location. SFRs may only be manipulated using direct addressing. Most assemblers (programs that convert assembly-language programs into machine code) allow use of the registers' names in place of their addresses.

The external memory space is shown in Figure 3–2. Code space may be split between internal and external ROM, depending on processor type and the logic level at the EA pin. External data space is always outside the microcontroller. Both code space and external data space may only be addressed indirectly, using the data pointer register as a pointer. It is also possible to use R0 or R1 as an indirect pointer to external data space addresses 0xFF or lower.

3–4   PROGRAM FLOW AND CONTROL

As described in Chapter 1, all microprocessors are essentially sequential devices. That is, they look at a list of instructions (the machine-code version of the program), and execute them one after the other until the power fails or they are told to stop. The register that keeps track of the list of instructions and which instruction comes next is the program counter (PC). The PC is a 16-bit register that always contains the address of the next instruction to be executed. The contents of the PC are used to output to the address bus at the beginning of the instruction cycle. As the current instruction is being executed, the

PC is adjusted to reflect the address of the next instruction in the list. The PC will be discussed further as it relates to branching instructions.

3–5   ASSEMBLY-LANGUAGE SOFTWARE

Addressing Modes

The 8051 family utilizes both direct and indirect addressing modes. Direct addressing is the most straightforward: The register or data cell being referenced contains the data to be used. An apt analogy is a mailbox. Your mailbox contains mail intended for you. When you go to get your mail, you go directly to your mailbox, which contains your mail. Similarly, when direct addressing is used, the microcontroller is provided with the address of the cell to be used.

A special form of direct addressing is immediate addressing, in which the microcontroller is given the data as a part of the instruction; it does not have to look in any cell or register. The data are provided as part of the instruction (i.e., the mail is put directly into your hand, so you never need to go to the mailbox).

In indirect addressing, however, the referenced register contains the address of the register or cell that actually contains the data to be used. Continuing the mailbox analogy, if you went to your mailbox and found a note telling you which other mailbox actually contained your mail, you would be indirectly addressing your mail. The closest you could get to your mail would be to look in your box for the address of the box containing your mail. In indirect addressing mode, the microcontroller is given the address of a cell that will contain the address of the cell containing the data to be used. In other words, the cell containing the address is used as a *pointer* to the real data. The use of pointers is especially important with tables of values, as will be seen later. Examples of the addressing modes will be presented with the programming examples.

The choice of addressing mode depends partially on the area of memory being addressed, partially on the instruction being used, and partially on the programmer's choice.

Assembly-Language Instructions

Assembly-language instructions for the 8051 family can be divided into three basic categories: data manipulation instructions; logical and mathematical instructions; and branching and flow control instructions. Although most instructions will work with both addressing modes (indirect and direct) and with most registers, there are limitations.

In general, instructions take the form:

opcode   operand

The opcode is a binary representation of an instruction such as MOVe (MOV) or JuMP (JMP), which tells the CPU which operation to perform. The operand provides additional data that may be needed by the CPU in order to know what to move or where to jump. The operand may be composed of one or two pieces of data. These data are usually referred to as the **destination** and the **source.**

The destination tells the CPU where to put the result of the operation, and the source denotes where the CPU is expected to find the data to be used. Some instructions implicitly define either the source or the destination or both, reducing the need for more than one piece of data in the operand. Refer to the Intel or Signetics manuals (see the Introduction) for the details and the syntactical limits of each instruction. Each category of instructions is described as follows and is shown by example.

Data Manipulation Instructions.   Data manipulation instructions are used to move data from one location to another. The term ''move'' is actually a misnomer, since in reality the data byte is copied to the new location, leaving the byte intact at the source location. The generalized form of the move instruction is

$$MOV \qquad y,x$$

The MOV instruction takes data from location x (the source) and copies it to location y (the destination). In this case x and y may be immediate data, memory locations such as R7 or 0x20, or indirect addresses. Figure 3–3 is an example program showing many of the data move instructions and demonstrating the form of an assembly-language program.

The program shown is not designed to thoroughly test the functionality of the internal and external data memory. It is an abbreviated test for use as a program example. The status of the test is shown on port 1 by the condition of the bits. See Figure 3–4.

A basic understanding of the function of the program is important to understanding of the instructions being explained. The program tests the internal and external memory in the following manner (line numbers refer to program lines in Figure 3–3):

1. Clear the output port in order to reset the ''bad memory'' bits (line 2). Immediate data 00h is MOVed to SFR P0.
2. Set bit 3 of the output port high to indicate the beginning of the internal RAM test (line 3).
3. Test R0 first, since it is to be used as a pointer. R0 is tested by writing 0xA5 to it (MOVing immediate data 0xA5 into R0) and then checking via a subtraction that the value in R0 is really 0xA5. If R0 is found to be bad, port 1, bit 0, is set (lines 4 through 9).
4. Test internal RAM nondestructively [i.e., save the contents and then restore them following the test (lines 10 through 17)]. R0 is used as an indirect pointer to the internal memory as well as the loop counter for this test. The test procedure is:
   a. Save the contents of the location to be tested in register B (line 11).
   b. Write 0xAA to the location to be tested (line 12).
   c. Check to see that 0xAA is really in the location (line 13).
   d. Restore the contents of the location (line 14).
   Finally, decrement R0 (the loop counter and test location address) and repeat the test for the next lower location (line 15). Should any location not test good, set port 1, bit 0, as an indicator (line 17).
5. Clear bit 3 and set bit 4 to mark the end of the internal RAM test and beginning of the external RAM test (lines 18 and 19).
6. Lines 20 through 35 test the external memory in exactly the same manner. The data pointer is used as the indirect pointer and loop counter in much the same manner as

```
 1            org     0000h              ;starting addr for code
 2 init:     mov     P1,#00h            ;clear P1
 3 restart:  setb    P1.3               ;mark beginning of int test
 4           mov     R0,#0a5h           ;test R0 by writing...
 5           mov     A,#0a5h            ;and comparing content.
 6           clr     C                  ;clear for subtract
 7           subb    A,R0               ;compare by subtraction
 8           jz      testint            ;jump if good
 9           setb    P1.0               ;set bad flag if bad
10 testint:  mov     R0,#7fh            ;set highest int mem loc.
11 intloop:  mov     b,@R0              ;save contents of ram loc.
12           mov     @R0,#0aah          ;write to ram loc.
13           cjne    @R0,#0aah,badint   ;check loc.
14           mov     @R0,b              ;restore contents of loc.
15           djnz    R0,intloop         ;continue test
16           sjmp    testext            ;to to ext test when done
17 badint:   setb    P1.0               ;mark if bad memory
18 testext:  clr     P1.3               ;unmark int test bit
19           setb    P1.4               ;mark external test bit
20           mov     DPTR,#0000h        ;point to first test loc
21 extloop:  movx    A,@DPTR            ;save contents....
22           mov     B,A                ;in B
23           mov     A,#0aah            ;test code to write
24           movx    @DPTR,A            ;write to memory loc.
25           movx    a,@DPTR            ;read memory loc.
26           cjne    a,#0aah,badext     ;compare for bad
27           mov     A,B                ;restore loc. contents
28           movx    @DPTR,a            ;write to mem loc.
29           inc     DPTR               ;point to next location
30           mov     A,DPH              ;check for done.......
31           orl     A,DPL              ;by looking for zero
32           jnz     extloop            ;jump back if not done
33           sjmp    extok              ;jump to end of ext. test
34 badext:   setb    P1.7               ;mark external memory bad
35 extok:    clr     P1.4               ;clear external test bit
36           sjmp    restart            ;go back and repeat test
37           end
```

FIGURE 3–3 Assembly-code memory test program.

FIGURE 3–4 Memory test program status byte.

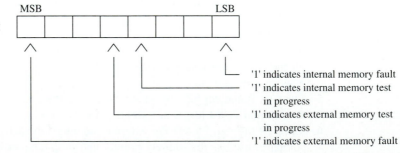

'1' indicates internal memory fault

'1' indicates internal memory test in progress

'1' indicates external memory test in progress

'1' indicates external memory fault

R0 was used to test the internal RAM. Line 34 sets port 1, bit 7, should any location test bad.

7. Finally, clear the external bit to signify the end of external test (line 36) and restart the program.

The output from the program in Figure 3–4 should provide a high level on P1.3 during the internal memory test and a high level on P1.4 during the external memory test. These pulses may be timed using an oscilloscope to determine the actual length of the tests. Relating to the hardware section, it can also be observed that the $\overline{RD}$ and $\overline{WR}$ control lines pulse only during the external memory test. Figure 3–5 shows the resulting waveforms with timing for an 80C31.

The test program also shows a number of data manipulation instructions being applied. For instance, line 2 is an example of direct addressing and the use of immediate data. In this line, the value 0x00 is copied to port 1. The port is a direct address and the 0x00 is immediate data. The actual form of the instruction found in the INTEL or Signetics data books is

MOV   direct,data

As shown, "direct" is the direct address in internal RAM (in this case an SFR address) of P1, and "data" is a byte-size number that is to be moved (actually copied) to P1. In this case the "direct" is the destination and "data" is the source. Data always flow from the source to the destination. In other words, the left-most part of the operand is the destination and the right-most portion is the source.

The internal memory test loop (lines 11 through 16) show indirect addressing using R0 as the address pointer. The contents of R0 are used as the address for the data manipulation. Indirect addressing is established by the "@" sign preceding R0. Only R0 and R1 may be used as indirect address pointers.

External memory is tested using a similar loop in lines 21 through 34. The data pointer (DPTR) SFR is loaded with the starting address in line 20 (a 16-bit immediate MOV instruction), which is then incremented as the test proceeds by the increment instruction in line 29. Indirect addressing is used in lines 21, 24, 25, and 28 (note the

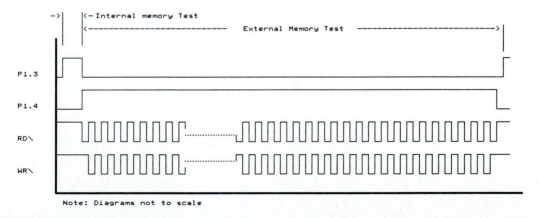

Note: Diagrams not to scale

FIGURE 3–5 Memory test timing.

''@'' with the DPTR), with the DPTR acting as the pointer to external memory. External code and data memory may only be addressed indirectly using the DPTR. Only the accumulator may be used as a source or destination operand for external data transfers. The external test loop is therefore somewhat longer than the internal memory test loop, since moving data in and out of external memory may only be accomplished by first moving data into or out of the accumulator.

Logical and Mathematical Instructions.   The logical instructions provide the facility to perform bitwise ANDs, ORs, eXclusive ORs, ROTate, and nibble SWAPping in the accumulator. The logical instructions work in a bitwise fashion. This means that the source byte is logically combined with the destination byte and the result placed in the destination location. As an example, consider line 31 in Figure 3–3. The instruction calls for the contents of the DPTR low byte (source) to be logically ORd with the contents of the accumulator and the result to be placed in the accumulator (destination). Executing this instruction with the A register containing 0x12 and the DPL register containing 0x48 would leave 0x5a in the A register. DPL would be unchanged. Lines 30 and 31 together are used to check when the DPTR reaches zero.

The mathematical instructions allow for ADDition, SUBtraction, MULtiplication, and DIVision as well as INCrementing and DECrementing values.

The program shown in Figure 3–6 uses the logical and mathematical instructions to read port P3 and to display the product of the upper and lower nibbles of P3 on P1 and the quotient of dividing the upper nibble of P3 by the lower nibble of P3 on P2 and the remainder from the division on P0.

Examples of logical instructions are shown in lines 4, 7, and 8 of the program in Figure 3–6. The accumulator is the destination register for all logical instructions. Logical (bitwise) ANDs with immediate data are shown in lines 4 and 8 in Figure 3–6. It is also legitimate to AND the contents of two registers or two SFRs together.

```
 1             org      0000h    ;starting addr for code
 2  start:     mov      R0,P3    ;read input from P3
 3             mov      A,R0     ;move input data to A
 4             anl      A,#0fh   ;mask off upper nybble
 5             mov      R1,a     ;save lower nybble data
 6             mov      A,R0     ;move input data back to A
 7             swap     A        ;exchange nybbles
 8             anl      A,#0fh   ;mask off the lower nybble
 9             mov      R2,A     ;save upper nybble data
10             mov      B,R1     ;move lower nybble to B...
11             mul      AB       ;and multiply by the upper nybble
12             mov      P1,A     ;output results
13             mov      B,R1     ;move lower nybble to B...
14             mov      A,R2     ;and upper nybble to A....
15             div      AB       ;to divide upper by lower
16             mov      P2,A     ;display integer result on P2...
17             mov      P0,b     ;and remainder on P0
18             sjmp     start    ;repeat forever
19             end
```

FIGURE 3–6 Logical and mathematical program example.

Line 4 shows the use of the AND instruction to *mask* unwanted bits. In this case the lower nibble needs to be separated from the byte. The masking technique is to AND the unwanted bits with 0 (anything ANDed with 0 is always 0) in order to force the unwanted bits to 0. The desired bits are left in their original states by ANDing them with 1s (any bit ANDed with 1 leaves the bit unchanged). In this way the unwanted bits are changed to 0 and the useful bits are left unchanged.

An example of the swap instruction is shown in line 7. The swap instruction exchanges the upper and lower nibbles of the A register. In other words, if the A register contains 0x1f before the SWAP is executed, it will contain 0xf1 after the instruction is executed. SWAP works only with the accumulator, but like all 8051 assembly-code mnemonics, it requires an operand (in this case A) to be stated explicitly.

Multiply and divide instructions are also shown in Figure 3–6. These two instructions work only with the A and B registers. The operand for the multiply and divide instructions is always AB (no spaces or punctuation). In the case of the multiply instruction, the value in A is multiplied by the value in B. The result is a 16-bit number placed in A and B, with the most significant byte in B and the least significant byte in A. For example, placing 0x5 in A and 0x6 in B before executing the multiply instruction will result in 0x1e in A and 0x00 in B. Line 11 of the example program shows the multiply instruction in use.

The divide instruction is very similar to the multiply instruction (see line 15 in Figure 3–6). In this case, the number in the A register is divided by the number in the B register. The integer result is placed in A and the remainder is placed in B. For example, placing 0x30 in A and 0x9 in B will result in a 5 in A (the integer result of 0x30/0x8) and a 3 in B (the remainder from the division). The division instruction is shown in line 15.

Branching and Flow Control Instructions. Branching instructions alter the flow of the sequence of the instructions being executed. If no branching instructions are encountered, the microcontroller executes its instructions one after the other in the order they occur in memory. It is often necessary for the program to branch, or alter the flow, as the mechanism to make decisions. The branching and flow control instructions include jumps, conditional jumps, and calls. Branching instructions accomplish the change of program flow by altering the contents of the PC. The PC is output to the address bus at the beginning of each instruction cycle as the address of the instruction to be fetched and executed, so any changes to the PC will affect the flow of the program by changing the source address for the next instruction.

Branching instructions may be unconditional or conditional. Unconditional branches alter the program flow no matter what other conditions may exist. An analogy is the "go to jail" card in the popular board game. The branch to your flow through the program is unequivocally altered (you cannot get out of it) by the unconditional branch instruction (the program equivalent of the "go to jail, do not pass go, do not collect $200" card).

Conditional branching occurs only if a condition is true. The same analogy could be used if you draw a "pay poor tax or go to jail" card. If you can pay the tax (the condition is met), then your flow is not altered. If you cannot pay the tax, then the branch to jail occurs.

Unconditional branches are accomplished by simply modifying the value in the PC. Conditional jumps in the 8051 instruction set depend on the results of a previous operation or the current value of a register or SFR to determine whether a branch will occur (whether the PC is altered).

Three types of jumps (the usual branching instruction) are used with the 8051: long jumps, absolute jumps, and relative jumps. The reason for the three types is to save code memory space. The long jump is a jump to an absolute address anywhere in the 64K code space. It has the form

JMP   address

The JMP is the instruction and the address is the 16-bit address to which the branch should occur. This instruction requires 3 bytes of machine-code space. It functions by simply loading the PC with the address given in the instruction. When the next instruction is fetched for execution, it will come from the changed address given by the PC and the branch will have occurred.

The absolute branches and relative branches are similar in that they depend on the current contents of the PC and jump relative to this current value. In order to use the current value in the PC, it is important to remember that the PC contains the address of the next instruction to be executed. For example, while line 12 of Figure 3–6 is executing, the PC contains the address of the instruction in line 13.

The absolute jumps leave the contents of the PC bits 11, 12, 13, 14, and 15 unchanged and replace the lower 11 bits from the data in the instruction. In this way a jump can occur to any address within the current 2K page of code memory. Since the new address bits 0 through 7 are in a data byte and bits 8 through 10 are included in the instruction opcode, the absolute jump is a 2-byte instruction.

Relative jumps function by adding the data byte from the instruction in a signed binary manner to the PC. In this way a relative jump can branch forward 127 bytes or backward 128 bytes from the contents of the PC (the address of the next instruction to be executed). In order to minimize program size, one unconditional jump and all the conditional jumps are relative jumps.

Examples of a number of branching instructions are shown in Figure 3–7. The short jumps (lines 10, 23, and 31) are examples of unconditional branching. Examples of conditional branching occur in lines 3, 8, 19, 29, and 31. In each case, if the condition is true, the branch will occur.

The JNZ (Jump if accumulator is Not Zero) instruction is an example of an instruction that uses the current content of the accumulator to make a branching decision. In this case, if the current contents of the accumulator is Not Zero, the branch will occur. The JC (Jump if Carry set) instruction in line 19 depends in a similar manner on the contents of the carry flag bit for its branching decision.

Processor flags are bits contained in the processor status word (PSW) SFR. The flag bits are bits 7, 6, and 2, which are the Carry (C) flag, Auxiliary Carry (AC) flag, and Overflow (O) flag, respectively. These bits reflect the result of the most recent mathematical or logical instruction that was executed. The carry flag is set if there was a carry generated (the result of the previous operation exceeded 8 bits), the auxiliary carry flag is set if there was a carry from bit 3 to bit 4, and the overflow flag is set if there was a carry from bit 6 to bit 7 or a carry from bit 7 but not from bit 6. The overflow flag is used for

```
 1              org     2000h
 2    wait:     mov     A,P2        ;read Port 2
 3              cjne    A,#00,wait  ;wait for P2=0
 4    cheq:     mov     A,P2        ;read P2 for value
 5              mov     R0,A        ;store in R0
 6              swap    A           ;exchange nybbles
 7              xrl     A,R0        ;check for zero
 8              jnz     noteq       ;jump if not equal
 9              mov     P1,#18h     ;output code for equal
10              sjmp    delay       ;go wait a bit
11    noteq:    mov     A,P2        ;reread P2 value
12              anl     A,#0fh      ;mask upper nybble
13              mov     R0,A        ;save lower nybble
14              mov     A,P2        ;reread Port 2
15              swap    A           ;exchange nybbles
16              anl     A,#0fh      ;mask lower nybble
17              clr     C           ;clear Carry for subtraction
18              subb    A,R0        ;if upper>lower then set C
19              jc      uphigh      ;jump if upper>lower
20    lowhigh:  mov     A,P1        ;read current port value
21              rl      A           ;rotate left 1 bit
22              mov     P1,a        ;output new value
23              sjmp    delay       ;go wait a bit
24    uphigh:   mov     A,P1        ;read current port value
25              rr      A           ;rotate 1 bit right
26              mov     P1,A        ;output new value
27    delay:    mov     R0,#0ffh    ;outter loop delay value
28    oloop:    mov     R1,#0ffh    ;inner loop delay value
29    iloop:    djnz    R1,iloop    ;wait through inner loop
30              djnz    R0,oloop    ;wait through outter loop
31              sjmp    cheq        ;repeat cycle
32              end
```

FIGURE 3–7 Branching instructions example.

signed arithmetic, where bit 7 is treated as the sign bit. Each of these flags will be set or cleared to reflect the results of the most recent instruction that affected the flags. The instructions that affect the flags and which flags they affect are detailed in the INTEL and Signetics manuals. Using an addition instruction will demonstrate the flag bits.

An example is to add 0x88 to 0x8c. The following instructions are used:

MOV   A,#8ch ;load A with 0x8c

ADD   A,#88h ;add 0x88 to 0x80

Mathematically, the problem is worked as follows:

```
Carry:      1    1
              10001100
              10001000
            100010100
```

The result is A = 0x14, because the A register is only 8 bits wide. The auxiliary carry flag is set because there is a carry generated from the addition of the lower nibbles, and the overflow flag is cleared because there is no carry generated by the addition of the lower 7 bits (and no carry from bit 6). The carry flag is set because the results are greater than 8 bits (a carry is generated by the addition of the two values).

Lines 3, 29, and 30 show the more complex but convenient conditional branching instructions. The CJNE (Compare and Jump if Not Equal) instruction is used in line 4 to create a wait loop until P1 is found to be set to zero. The CJNE combines the functions of a CoMPare (a normal microprocessor instruction not present in the 8051 instruction set) and a JNZE (Jump if Not Zero or Equal) instruction. The CJNE compares the values at the time the instruction is executed. This is a convenient combination of instructions, which is in fact necessary since the 8051 has no CoMPare instruction and no zero flag on which to base a subsequent branching decision. The convenience is somewhat tempered by the fact that there is no corollary CJE instruction and by limitations on the registers that may be used with CJNE.

The DJNZ (Decrement and Jump if the result is Not Zero) instruction (lines 29 and 30) is very convenient for software loops. It performs both the decrement of the target register and the check for a zero result in one step. The DJNZ is very flexible (although not unlimited) in its application to registers and memory variables. In the example program in Figure 3–7, the DJNZ is used to implement a dual-loop time delay in lines 28 through 31. Although this is not necessarily the best way to implement a time delay, it is an effective use of the DJNZ instruction. Figure 3–3, the memory test program, shows the DJNZ instruction in line 15. In this example, the DJNZ is actually decrementing the indirect address pointer as well as controlling the number of times the loop is executed.

CALL instructions are branching instructions used to execute subroutines. Subroutines are portions of a program that are going to be used from several places in the program. For example, a routine to read a byte on port 1 may need to be used at several different points in the program. By writing the port read code as a subroutine, the program can CALL it from anywhere in the program. A brief example of a subroutine is as follows.

Main program:
  —code line x
  —code line y
  call subber
  —code line z
  —code line a

Subroutine code:
  subber: —subroutine code line 1
          —subroutine line 2
          .
          .
    ret

When the CALL instruction is executed, the program branches to the subroutine and executes the code of the subroutine until it executes a RETurn instruction, which then causes the program to branch back to the point at which the call occurred. The CALL instruction used with subroutines takes two forms: The LCALL (Long CALL) is an instruction that can call a subroutine anywhere in the 64K code space; the ACALL (Absolute CALL) instruction can call a subroutine that is located within the 2K page of memory in which the call occurred.

The **stack** is an important element relative to subroutines. The stack is an area of memory used by the CPU for temporary storage of data. It is a LIFO (last-in, first-out) storage area. An important use for the stack is to store the return address for a subroutine call. When the CALL instruction executes, the contents of the PC (the next address to be executed after the call instruction) is stored on the stack. Thus 2 bytes (the address of the next instruction) are pushed onto the stack. The stack is controlled by an SFR called the stack pointer (SP). The SP contains the address of the last byte stored on the stack and defaults to 0x07 upon reset. When a byte is to be added to the stack, the SP is incremented and the byte is then stored at the location given by the SP. In the case of a call instruction, this process is repeated twice for the 2 bytes in the address (bytes stored at 0x08 and 0x09 in this example). Later, when the RETurn instruction is executed, the opposite actions occur to pop 2 bytes from the stack and replace them into the PC. In this way execution continues from the instruction following the CALL after the subroutine has completed its task.

The stack may also be used with caution by the programmer. The PUSH and POP instructions store and retrieve bytes from the stack. Caution must be exercised, however, because the stack is a LIFO device. Data pushed onto the stack during the execution of a subroutine must be popped off the stack before exiting the subroutine, so that the RETurn instruction retrieves the correct return address from the stack.

The last category of instructions are the Boolean or bit-oriented instructions. These have been referred to earlier but need further clarification. They are among the major conveniences of the 8051 family assembly language.

Boolean instructions relate to the use of or modification of bit-size data. They can deal with a single data bit. The simplest of these are the SETB (SET Bit high) and CLR (CLeaR) instructions. These two instructions allow manual control of a bit's state. The bit being affected must have a bit-addressable direct address. In a non–controller-oriented micro (8085, 8086, Z80, etc.), the need to set or clear a single bit is a multiple-step process. As an example, consider the following steps used to create a positive-going pulse on bit 3 of port 1 without disturbing the other bits of the port:

1. Read the current contents of the port.
2. Use an OR instruction to set bit 3 high.
3. Output the value to the port.
4. Use an AND instruction to force bit 3 low.
5. Output the value to the port.

The following code will make the same pulse on an internal port of an 8051 family controller:

1. SETB   P1.3
2. CLR   P1.3

Other Boolean instructions allow the programmer to ComPLement (CPL) a bit, do a Logical ANd (ANL) or a Logical OR (ORL), or move (MOV) a bit provided that either the source or the destination bit is the Carry bit.

Finally, Boolean conditional jumps allow branching that depends on the condition of a bit. The JC (Jump on Carry set) instruction is shown in Figure 3–7, line 19. The other Boolean conditional relative branches are more generalized and can be used to test a number of different bits including port bits. These are the JB (Jump if Bit set), JNB (Jump if Bit Not set), and JBC (Jump if Bit set and Clear bit) instructions. The Boolean processing capabilities are probably the single feature that most exemplifies a microcontroller as opposed to a general-purpose microprocessor.

Some microprocessors also contain special instructions for I/O. These do not exist in the 8051 instruction set. As far as programming is concerned, the ports internal to the 8051 controller are just more SFRs. Further I/O ports, if needed, must be memory mapped and are therefore treated as memory locations. These are then mapped into the external data space and are addressed indirectly using the DPTR and the MOVX instruction. Refer to Figure 3–3, lines 21, 24, and 25.

3–6   HIGH-LEVEL, STRUCTURED LANGUAGES

High-level, structured languages such as C, Forth, PL/M, and BASIC are all available for the 8051 family, typically in the form of cross-compilers—language compilers that run on a host computer such as a personal computer and produce code that can be executed by an 8051 family controller. BASIC for the 8051 is available in a cross-compiler version but is more commonly available in an interpreter version for execution directly on the 8051 or on the 8052. The use of a high-level language relieves the programmer of many details associated with assembly language but also removes control of the code from the programmer. The result is usually more bytes of code to do the same job.

Figure 3–8 shows the program of Figure 3–7 translated into C for the 8051. Although there may be more compact methods to implement some of the functions shown in Figure 3–7, a fairly direct translation is shown to permit comparisons.

Table 3–2 compares the two programs. It is apparent that the C language is much easier to write (12 lines as opposed to 31 lines of assembly code). However, the machine code produced by the C compiler is more than twice as long. The implication of longer

```
data unsigned char lnybble, unybble;
data unsigned int i;

main()
  {
  while (P3 != 0);  /* wait for P3 = 0*/
  while (1)
    {
    lnybble = (P3 & 0x0f); /*get lower nybble*/
    unybble =((P3 & 0xf0) >> 4); /*get lower nybble*/
    if (lnybble == unybble) P1 = 0x18; /*output equal code*/
    if (lnybble > unybble) P1 = (P1 >> 1); /*shift right*/
    if (lnybble < unybble) P1 = (P1 << 1); /*shift left*/
    if ((P1 == 0x80) || (P1 == 0x01)) P1 = (P1 | 0x81); /*clean up*/
    if (P1 == 0x02) P1 = 0x03; /*more clean up*/
    if (P1 == 0x40) P1 = 0xc0; /*all cleaned up*/
    for (i=0; i<=3200; i++); /*delay*/
```

FIGURE 3–8   C program example.

TABLE 3–2 Program comparison

	Assembly Language	C Language
Lines of code	31	12
Program length (bytes)	53	114

code is that it would execute more slowly. In these examples execution speed is actually of no importance, since a long delay is included in the program; but if time were critical, assembly language would be required.

3–7 PROGRAM DEVELOPMENT

Assemblers and Compilers

An **assembler** is a program that takes the assembly-language program and assembles it into machine language for use by the microcontroller. **Compilers** do the same job for high-level languages such as C. With both assemblers and compilers, the steps to create the machine language program are similar:

1. Use an editor to create a source program. The source program is a plain-text file of the assembly-language instructions or the high-level language commands.
2. Use the assembler program (or the compiler when using high-level languages) to create a machine-language program for the microcontroller. Typically a ''list'' file will also be created, showing the assembled (or compiled) version of the program. Most of the program examples included here are actually list files.

   Unfortunately, the assembler or compiler programs will sometimes discover some syntactical errors when the program is first compiled or assembled. In the case of such errors, it is necessary to return to step 1 to modify the source file to correct the errors. Steps 1 and 2 are repeated until the assembler or compiler reports that no syntactical errors exist.
3. The machine language may now be loaded into the microcontroller for testing. If the program does not work correctly, modify the source code and repeat steps 1, 2, and 3 until the program works correctly.

Assemblers and compilers vary in their requirements for the form of the source code. In general, assemblers and compilers require further information (in addition to the program itself). In assemblers these extra instructions are called assembler directives; in compilers they are called switches or controls. The manner in which the source code is laid out will affect execution speed and machine-language program size.

Program Structure

Program development with embedded controllers requires a structured approach to programming. Memory limitations make it important to control the size of the program code.

TABLE 3–3   Program structures

Item	Assembly Language	C Language
Assembler/compiler information	Equates ORG JMP to main program	Defines Include files
Functions/subroutine code	Interrupt service routines Subroutines (no forward calls)	Interrupt functions Functions (no forward calls)
Main program code	Initializations Main program code	Initializations Main program code

The variety of branching modes (short, absolute, and long) provided by the 8051 family make the size of the final code relate strongly to the structure of the source program. Examples of suggested structures are shown in Table 3–3.

Most assemblers and, to a lesser extent, compilers assign addresses in the order that the source program code is read. Assemblers also typically allow the use of a generic CALL or JMP without a designation of Short, Long, or Absolute. The assembler chooses the correct jump as it assembles the code.

Similarly, compilers put executable code into a program as they read each line of source code. Consequently, it is important for the assembler or compiler to find the subroutines or functions first, so it can assign starting addresses to these and be able to use short or absolute branches where possible. If the compiler or assembler does not yet know the starting address of a function when it finds a reference to it, then a long branch (a 3-byte instruction) must be used since there is no way for the assembler or compiler to determine the best form of the instruction.

Development Systems

Development systems allow a designer to develop and test software in conjunction with the hardware as part of the development process. Assuming that the hardware already exists, there are two major steps in the development process, software development and software/hardware debugging. Figure 3–9 shows the development cycle in flowchart form. At each step of the process, errors are corrected before proceeding.

The overall purpose of the development process is to produce working 8051-based project software. The process first involves creating error-free machine code in the software development phase (assembling or compiling). The resulting code is "error free" only in the sense that the language assembler or language compiler has produced valid machine code that is free of syntactical errors.

After the software is created and either compiled or assembled into machine code, it may be tested using a simulator or by loading it into the processor and running the program. These are part of the software/hardware debugging phase of the development process.

The hardware/software debugging phase usually consists of actually running the hardware to test operation. It can be handled in several ways. The first and least convenient method is to program an EPROM with the code and run the project. This is a quick

FIGURE 3–9 Development process.

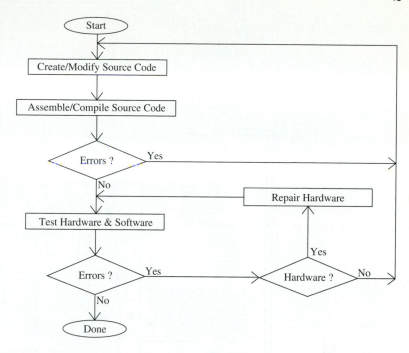

method to get started but is usually much slower in the long run. The "burn and try" method isolates the designer from really seeing what the processor is doing at points in the program. The designer must guess where the program is going wrong, then change the code or the hardware and then reburn and retry.

An improvement over "burn and try" is to use a monitor program running on the 8051 that will allow the program code to be downloaded (usually serially) and run. A monitor program is a simple program that the processor runs in order to be able to load and execute programs for test purposes. A simple monitor will only provide a means to download and execute program code, whereas a full-featured monitor will also allow manipulation of memory contents and a breakpoint (a program debugging aid) facility to assist in analyzing problems. A simple monitor program is presented in Chapter 4.

The 8051 presents a unique problem in using a monitor for downloading. The code memory space and the data memory space are separate. The machine code that is downloaded must be written into external data space, because there are no instructions to write to code space. The solution to the problem is to make a portion of memory active in both code space and external data space. In other words, the physical memory chip appears to the processor to be both external data memory and code memory. Figure 3–10 shows the project presented in Chapter 2 as modified for use with a downloading monitor.

The modifications are (1) to add AND gate U11A, and (2) to move the connections to the U7 outputs "up" one output (move each device to a higher address). The AND gate performs the function of causing U4 (the RAM) to respond when either code space or external data space is being used. Both the $\overline{PSEN}$ and the $\overline{RD}$ are active low, so when both are high the output is high to U4 (the inactive state for U4). During a code space access, PSEN goes low, causing the output of U11 to go low and activate U4 to respond.

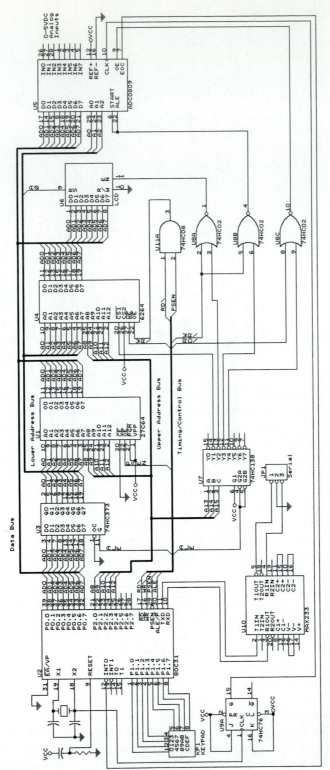

FIGURE 3–10 Monitor-based project.

Likewise, during an external memory space access, RD goes low, and the output of U11 goes low, activating U4. U4 will actually be activated as described above *only* if its address is currently on the address bus.

The fact that U4 is now responding in both code and external data space is the reason for the change at U7. The address range for U4 was 0–0x1FFF. A bus conflict will result if more than one device responds at a single address. Because U4 now responds in both code and external data spaces, it cannot share addresses with U1.

The modified memory map in Figure 3–11 shows clearly that U4 is accessible in either code space or external data space. This code may be downloaded into U4 as external data and then run from U4 as code. The only problem with this scheme is that the code to be executed must be assembled or compiled to reside in the space available to U4. For assembly code, this is handled by an ORG statement. For high-level languages, it usually means that a dummy assembly code module must be linked in during the link/locate phase of compilation. The exact method used will depend on the compiler.

Using a monitor can present some challenges (not insurmountable) when using interrupts and other advanced techniques. These can be avoided through the use of other development tools. Tools such as emulators, ROMulators, and on-screen simulators can provide valuable help if the project budget will support them.

Emulators are devices that will plug into the processor socket on a development project and emulate the processor. Usually they are run from another computer such as a personal computer. Emulators allow the program to be tested by first loading the code into the emulator and then executing the code through the emulator. The emulator can then control the speed of emulation and display of the status of the processor during the emulation. Troubleshooting of software and hardware is greatly simplified through the use of an emulator. The drawback to emulators are their cost and the training time needed to apply them efficiently.

A less costly option to an emulator is a ROMulator. This device accepts downloaded code and then appears to be the system ROM to the processor. Many of the diagnostic tools available with an emulator are not available in a ROMulator, but the cost is less.

Both the emulator and the ROMulator use the actual project hardware to exercise and test the program. Sometimes the hardware is simply not available, or safety reasons

FIGURE 3–11 Modified memory map.

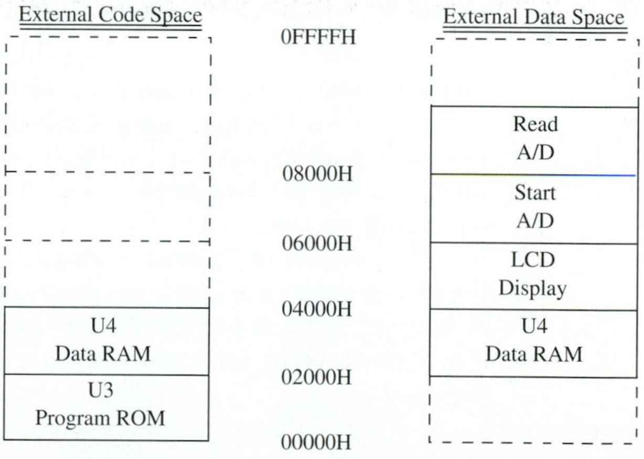

preclude the use of real hardware. In these cases an on-screen simulator may be used to test and debug the software without hardware.

On-screen simulators run on a personal computer and simulate the actions of an 8051 processor. Screen displays show the contents of ports, SFRs, registers, and memory locations as the program "executes." By carefully observing the results on the ports or other I/O devices (as shown on the screen), it is fairly easy to debug a program to the point where it is virtually guaranteed to work on actual hardware.

3-8   SUMMARY

This chapter presents the software issues associated with program development using 8051 embedded controllers. The 8051 microcontroller follows a sequential list of program instructions in binary form. The assembly-language instructions are written by the programmer, assembled into machine code, and stored in the nonvolatile program memory. The variety of instructions allow the programmer to create a program to accomplish almost any other task. The process of program development will lead to a functioning program.

3-9   EXERCISES

1. Write a fragment of assembly code to add the contents of R0 to the accumulator.
2. Which branching instructions will allow branching based on the contents of the accumulator?
3. Using the following starting conditions for *each* instruction,

$$A = 0x00 \qquad R1 = 0x06 \qquad PC = 0x2000$$

   calculate the contents of the PC after the instructions shown are executed.
   a. 0x2000   JMP   0x0030   PC = 0x _____
   b. 0x2010   SJMP   0x30   PC = 0x _____
   c. 0x4500   DJNZ   R1, −0x25   PC = 0x _____
4. Write an assembly-language program to fill internal RAM locations 0x20 through 0x30 with 0x00. Use only direct addressing and no loops.
5. Repeat Exercise 4 using a loop and indirect addressing.
6. Write a program to read port 1 and wait until bit 3 of port 1 is low before proceeding. After detecting the low on bit 3, set all of port 3 high and halt. Use masking to accomplish the task.
7. Write the program of Exercise 6 using Boolean instructions.
8. Use an assembler to assemble the results of Exercises 4 through 7. Make corrections as necessary until all syntactical errors are cleared.
9. Use a simulator to verify the operation of each program created in Exercises 4 through 7.

CHAPTER 4

Built-In Peripherals

OVERVIEW

The 8051 family of microcontrollers includes a variety of peripherals in the package, among which are up to four 8-bit parallel ports, two counter/timers, and a serial port. Each of these devices is related to one or more SFR. In other words, the devices are initialized by setting the bits in the control SFRs and then monitoring device operation via status bits in the appropriate SFRs. This chapter explores the built-in peripherals of the 8051 family.

4–1   PARALLEL PORTS

Microprocessors use parallel ports to input or output bytes of data. The entire byte of data is either input from 8 lines simultaneously or output on 8 lines simultaneously. The 8 lines correspond to the 8 bits in the byte. In the case of the 8051 family, the ports may be used as byte-sized ports or as individual bits.

The internal parallel ports of the 8051 family function much like most microprocessor parallel ports except that the ports do not require initialization. That is, it is not necessary to configure the ports to be input or output (see Chapter 2 for details). The only requirement is that a port bit used for input must have a 1 written to its latch. The ports are usually addressed using their port designation shown as follows:

Assembly language:	mov p3, #34h	;write 34H to port 3
	mov a,p3	;read port 3
C language:	P3 = 0x34;	;write 34H to port 3
	x = P3;	;read port 3

These examples illustrate that reading from or writing to a port is accomplished simply by using the name of the port's SFR in the instruction. Most assemblers and compilers predefine the names of all the 8051 SFRs, so the programmer can simply use the SFR name as needed. The assembler or compiler then replaces the SFR's name with its direct address as it assembles or compiles the source code.

This section concentrates on example uses of the ports. In particular, a strobe-and-acknowledge handshake interface will be covered. This particular interface is common to printers and other parallel peripherals and illustrates the techniques of **handshaking.**

Handshaking is necessary whenever two devices are attempting to exchange data, unless the devices transfer data at identical rates. In handshaking, the slower device controls the rate of data transfer. For instance, a printer typically cannot print nearly as quickly as a computer can provide character data. Thus, the printer needs to be able to control the rate of data transfer so as not to be overrun with data.

The strobe-and-acknowledge handshake is a common form of handshaking for parallel data transfer. This type of handshake is implemented by having the slower device (e.g., the printer) acknowledge its readiness for each byte to be transferred. The computer asserts the data and follows with a strobe pulse to the printer. The computer then waits for an acknowledge pulse or level from the printer before asserting more data. The particular interface being described is shown in timing diagram form in Figure 4–1.

Figure 4–2 shows a program to print a message via a strobe-and-acknowledge interface. For this example the ports could be connected to a printer and the resulting message would be printed. Figure 4–3 shows a similar program in C language.

Comparing Figure 4–1, the timing diagram, and Figures 4–2 and 4–3, shows that the strobe-and-acknowledge interface occurs as follows: First the data to be transferred is output on port 1 (line 19 of Figure 4–2 and line 10 of Figure 4–3), then port 3, bit 3, is cleared and set to make the negative-going strobe pulse (lines 20 and 21 of Figure 4–2 and lines 11 and 12 of Figure 4–3). Finally, port 3, bit 4, is monitored until the acknowledge is received (line 22 of Figure 4–2 and line 13 of Figure 4–3). At this point the program proceeds and either outputs the next character if the message is incomplete or enters an infinite do-nothing loop after the twelfth character has been transferred. The do-nothing loop is included only as a way to halt execution while trying out the program.

These programs show examples of both byte-wide I/O and bit-oriented I/O. Line 19 of Figure 4–2 shows use of the 8051 ports for byte-size output. Lines 20, 21, and 22 of Figure 4–2 show I/O using single bits for input and for output.

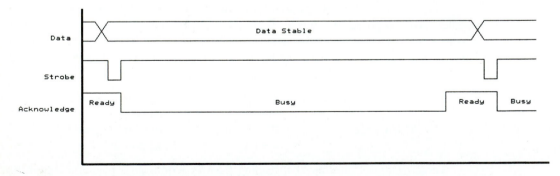

FIGURE 4–1   Strobe-and-acknowledge timing.

```
LINE        SOURCE
  1       ;Program to demonstrate a
  2       ;strobe-and-acknowldge handshake
  3       ;parallel data transfer.  Port 1
  4       ;transfers the data, Port 3, bit 3
  5       ;is the strobe and port 3 bit 2 is
  6       ;to input the acknowledge.
  7
  8       datap     equ     P1
  9       strobe    equ     P3.3
 10       ack       equ     P3.2
 11
 12
 13                 org     2000h
 14       init:     mov     dptr,#msg     ;point to string
 15                 mov     r0,#0         ;clear index counter
 16                 orl     P3,#0ch       ;set the strobe/ack high
 17       loop:     mov     a,r0          ;get the index
 18                 movc    a,@a+dptr     ;get character to print
 19                 mov     datap,a       ;output data
 20                 clr     strobe        ;start pulse
 21                 setb    strobe        ;finish pulse
 22        wait:    jnb     ack,wait      ;wait for ready
 23                 inc     r0            ;bump index
 24                 cjne    r0,#12,loop   ;12 characters printed?
 25       stay:     sjmp    stay          ;stay here
 26       msg:      db      'Hello world',0dh
 27                 end
```

FIGURE 4–2 Assembly-language strobe-and-acknowledge program.

```
stmt level    source

  1           #include <c:\c51\reg52.h>
  2
  3           data unsigned char x, i;
  4           code char msg [] = "Hello world\n" ;
  5
  6           main()
  7            {
  8     1       for (i=0; i<=11; i++) /*set up the loop*/
  9     1         {
 10     2         P1 = msg[i];   /*output character*/
 11     2         P3 = (P3 & 0xf7); /*negative edge of pulse*/
 12     2         P3 = (P3 | 0x08); /*positive edge of pulse*/
 13     2         while ((P3 & 0x4) == 0); /*wait for ready*/
 14     2         }
 15     1       while (1);  /*infinite loop*/
 16     1       }
```

FIGURE 4–3 C-language strobe-and-acknowledge program.

4–2   COUNTER/TIMER PERIPHERALS

Counter/timer peripherals are devices that can either use an internal or an external clock to measure time periods or that can be used to count events. These devices are usually configured as 16-bit ripple counters with one or more sources of input to the counter. A carry bit out of the counter is provided to indicate when rollover from 0xffff to 0x0000 has occurred. Example uses of counter/timer units are to measure a pulse width applied to the input of the counter/timer, to provide a specific frequency out of the counter/timer as an output from the microcomputer, or to provide a precise time delay within the program. For instance, a counter timer could be used to measure a pulse width or frequency as follows:

1. Set the timer/counter to 0x0000.
2. Start the timer/counter when the input pulse goes high.
3. Stop the timer/counter when the input pulse goes low.
4. Read the counters and use the clock frequency to calculate the pulse width or frequency of the input signal.

The counter/timers (''timers'') of the 8051 family are configured to be flexible and easy to apply. The timers are configured through two SFRs: TCON, the Timer CONtrol register; and TMOD, the Timer MODe register.

Figure 4–4 shows two different configurations for the counter portion of the timer/counter. The configuration is that of a 13- or 16-bit counter in modes 0 and 1, and of an 8-bit counter for mode 2. In mode 2 the 8-bit counter is automatically reloaded from the high-byte SFR each time it rolls over to 00.

Although the counter configuration may vary in details, the overall operation is the same for all modes. The counters are up counters (they count up each time a clock pulse is received), and the seventeenth bit of the counter, the timer flag (TFx, where x may be 0 or 1 depending on the counter being used) is set when the counter rolls over from all 1s to all 0s. The source of the pulses that are counted can be either from the system clock (crystal frequency) divided by 12 or from an external source. Either of the counter bytes can be written to (loaded) or read as required, since they are SFRs.

Three or four (depending on the counter) operating modes are available for the timers. Mode 0 is a 13-bit counter timer that emulates the timer in the 8048 processor. In this mode the low-byte counter functions as a 5-bit prescaler and the high-byte counter functions as an 8-bit up counter. Mode 1 is a straightforward 16-bit up counter, and mode 2 an 8-bit counter with auto-reload at the rollover point. In this latter mode, the lower byte does the counting and the contents of the high byte are loaded into the low byte at rollover.

Timer Operation

The contents of the TMOD and TCON SFRs determine the operating parameters for the timers; see Figure 4–5.

Timer operation is best understood by combining the information in Figures 4–4 and 4–5. The source of the pulses counted by each timer is selected by the $C/\overline{T}$ bit in the TMOD. If this bit is low (timer mode), the source is the system oscillator divided by 12. This is the configuration shown in Figure 4–4. Setting $C/\overline{T}$ high (counter mode)

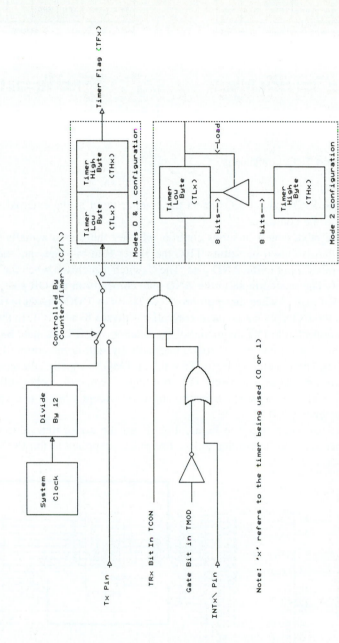

FIGURE 4-4 Timer/counter configuration.

53

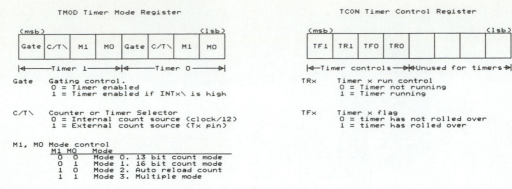

FIGURE 4-5   TMOD and TCON definitions.

causes the SPDT switch to connect the counter input to the external source, that is, the Tx pin on the controller.

The next switch in series controls whether the pulses actually reach the counter. This switch is closed by setting TRx, the Timer Run bit, high and then creating a logic 1 at the other input to the AND gate. The ''switch'' is closed when the AND gate outputs a logic 1. The second input to the AND gate comes from the OR gate, which will output the needed logic 1 when the appropriate GATE bit in TMOD is set to 0 (note the inverter) or when the INTx pin on the microcontroller is driven to a logic 1. In this way the external device connected to INTx can control the counter on/off if the gate bit is set high or else the counter on/off can be controlled internally by setting the correct GATE bit high and controlling the counter with the TRx bit in TMOD. Finally, the counter counts when pulses are applied to it and sets TFx to a logic 1 when the count rolls over from all 1s to 0s. The TFx bit must be cleared by software (except when it is used as an interrupt—see Chapter 6).

The example circuit in Figure 4-6 shows the use of timer 0 to measure the width of an incoming positive-going pulse. The pulse is applied to the INT0 pin of an 8031.

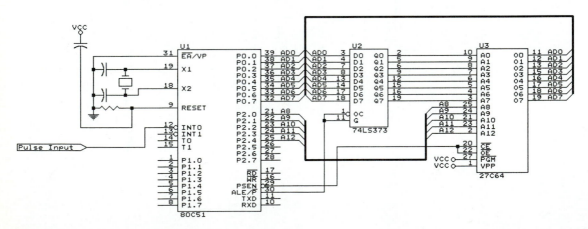

FIGURE 4-6   Timer example system.

```
1      pulse   equ     INT0
2
3              org     2000h
4      init:   mov     tmod,#09h    ;gate=1,mode 1
5              mov     tcon,#00h    ;clear all bits
6              setb    tr0          ;timer 0 on
7      loop:   jb      pulse,loop   ;wait for pulse low
8              clr     tf0          ;clear timer flag
9              mov     th0,#00      ;clear counters
10             mov     tl0,#00
11     waithi: jnb     pulse,waithi ;wait for pulse high
12     waitpl: jb      pulse,waitpl ;wait for pulse done
13             jb      tf0,loop     ;jump if rollover
14             mov     r0,tl0       ;get lsb of count
15             mov     r1,th0       ;get msb of count
16             sjmp    loop         ;go back for next pulse
17             end
```

FIGURE 4–7 Pulse measurement software (ASM).

In Figure 4–6, the pulse is applied to the INT0 pin so that it can be used to externally gate the clock pulses to the counter. The general count scheme is that the counter will be zeroed and the incoming pulse used to turn on the pulses to the counter. When the pulse is completed, the number of counts in the counter is proportional to the pulse width.

The software to measure the pulse width is shown in Figures 4–7 and 4–8. TCON and TMOD are loaded in the initialization phase of the programs. Timer 0 is configured

```
1          #include <c:\c51\reg52.h>
2
3          data unsigned char pulselow, pulsehigh;
4
5          main()
6            {
7     1     TMOD = 0x09;/* gate=1, mode 1*/
8     1     TCON = 0x00;/* clear all bits */
9     1     while (1)
10    1        {
11    2        TF0 = 0;/* clear timer flag */
12    2        while (INT0 == 1);/* wait for pulse low */
13    2        TR0 = 1;/* timer 0 on */
14    2        TH0 = 0x00;/* clear counters */
15    2        TL0 = 0x00;
16    2        while (INT0 == 0);/* wait while pulse low */
17    2        while (INT0 == 1);/* wait while pulse occurs */
18    2        if (TF0 == 0) /* check for rollover */
19    2           {
20    3           pulselow = TL0; /* save lsb of count */
21    3           pulsehigh = TH0;/* save msb of count */
22    3           }
23    2        }
24    1     }
```

FIGURE 4–8 Pulse measurement software (C).

as a mode 1 timer whose gate is controlled externally. In this way the counter is allowed to run and count the pulses from the internal clock only while the incoming pulse on INT0 is high.

The programs monitor the incoming pulse to assure that the input signal is at a logic low prior to clearing the counter registers. Then the programs wait for the pulse to occur by monitoring the INT0 pin. The INT0 pin serves as normal I/O and, at the same time, functions as the external gate control for timer 0. At the conclusion of the pulse, the counters are read and stored in memory. This program is really useful only to demonstrate the timer/counter, because the result ends up in memory. Further code is necessary to use the pulse width numbers stored in memory.

One should be able to calculate the actual width of the pulse being measured. The clock in the system of our example is set to 11.0592 MHz (the crystal), which is then divided by 12 to provide 921.6 kHz to the counters. This means that for each count found in the counters, 1.085 μs (1/921.6 kHz) have elapsed. Therefore, the actual pulse width can be found by multiplying the number found in the counters by 1.085 μs.

In order to use the 8031 in this manner, it is important to know the minimum and maximum pulse width that can be measured accurately. The resolution of the counter is the limiting factor for accuracy. The resolution is the smallest time increment that can be measured by the counter and is set by the counter clock. In this case the clock increment is 1.085 μs. If this counter setup were to be used to attempt to measure a 2-μs pulse, the chances of obtaining inaccurate results would be high. The accuracy depends on the ratio of the pulse width to be measured and the resolution of the counter. A good rule of thumb is that a minimum of 10 times the resolution is required for reasonable accuracy. In this case that would mean a 10% error is possible. Ten times the resolution would mean that a minimum pulse width of 10.85 μs (1.085 μs $\times$ 10) is required for accurate results. On the other end of the scale, the timer can count up to 65,535 counts before rolling over. The largest pulse that can be reliably measured is 71.11 ms (65535 $\times$ 1.085 μs). Pulses falling between 10.85 μs and 71.11 ms can be measured. If the software were modified to keep track of the number of times the timer rolled over, then much longer pulses could be measured.

Time Delays

Another use of timers is to provide time delays. A timer can be configured to provide a specific delay time by simply setting the starting count and then waiting for the TFx to indicate a rollover—the end of the time delay.

Figures 4–9 and 4–10 show delay subroutines. The programs rely on the fact that TMOD is correctly initialized by the main program. The routines each preload a count that is calculated to provide a specific time delay before rollover occurs. The timer 0 flag is then cleared and the timer 0 run bit is set to start the timer counting. The loop then waits for the timer flag to be set to indicate that rollover has occurred, that is, that the delay time (50 ms in this case) has elapsed. The loop counter (''x'' in the C program and ''b'' in the assembly program) is then decremented and the program makes another 50-ms delay or quits as indicated by the loop counter.

The numbers loaded into the counters determine the time delay for one time through the loop. The numbers are calculated in a manner similar to that shown for the pulse

```
1 delay:        mov    th0,#4ch      ;50 millisecs delay time
2               mov    tl0,#00h
3               clr    tf0           ;clear rollover flag
4               setb   tr0           ;turn on timer 0
5 tloop:        jnb    tf0,tloop     ;wait for rollover
6               clr    tr0           ;turn timer off
7               djnz   b,delay        ;loop until delay done
7               ret
```

FIGURE 4–9 Assembly-language time delay.

measurement example. The frequency driving the counters is still the system clock divided by 12 (11.0592 MHz ÷ 12 = 921.6 kHz), and so the time per count is 1/921.6 kHz = 1.085 μs. The major point to figuring the time delay is that the counters count *up* from the preset count to 0xffff before rolling over and setting the timer flag. Consequently, the number of counts necessary to produce a given delay must be subtracted from 0x10000 to determine the counter preload numbers. The calculations for the 50-ms delay are as follows:

$$\text{Counter clock frequency} = \frac{\text{system clock}}{12}$$

$$= \frac{11.0592\ \text{MHz}}{12} = 921.6\ \text{kHz}$$

$$\text{Time per clock count} = \frac{1}{\text{counter clock frequency}}$$

$$= \frac{1}{921.6\ \text{kHz}} = 1.085\ \mu\text{s}$$

$$\text{Counts for the delay} = \frac{\text{delay time}}{\text{time per clock count}}$$

$$= \frac{50\ \text{ms}}{1.085\ \mu\text{s}} = 46{,}080$$

$$\text{Preload count} = 0\text{x}10000 - \text{counts for the delay}$$
$$= 65{,}536 - 46{,}080 = 19{,}456 = 0\text{x}4\text{c}00$$

```
 1            void time(unsigned char fiftyms)
 2              {
 3     1        unsigned char x;
 4     1        for (x = 0; x < fiftyms; x++)
 5     1          {
 6     2          TH0 = 0x4c; /* 50 millisecond delay */
 7     2          TL0 = 0x00;
 8     2          TF0 = 0;    /* clear rollover flag */
 9     2          TR0 = 1;    /* turn timer on */
10     2          while (TF0 == 0); /* wait for roll over */
11     2          TR0 = 0;    /* timer off */
12     2          }
13     1          }
```

FIGURE 4–10 C-language time delay.

These calculations indicate that the counters need to count 46,080 counts to use up 50 ms. The counters are preloaded 46,080 counts below 65,536, so that it will take 50 ms for the counters to count up to 65,535 (0xffff) and then roll over to 0000 on the next count. At that point the timer flag will be set to indicate that the delay is complete.

Mode 2 is the 8-bit auto-reload mode, and it is most useful for producing a series of repeating pulses. In the next section, mode 2 is used to provide the clock for the serial port. The reload rate on the timer establishes the baud rate of the serial communications. Later, in Chapter 6, mode 2 is used to provide variable pulse width drive.

4–3   SERIAL COMMUNICATIONS

Serial communication is often used either to control or to receive data from an embedded microcomputer. Serial communication is a form of I/O in which the bits of a byte being transferred appear one after the other in a timed sequence on a single wire. Serial communication has become the standard for intercomputer communication.

The example serial waveforms in Figure 4–11 show the waveform on a single conductor to transmit a byte (0x41) serially. The upper waveform is the TTL-level waveform seen at the transmit pin of the microcontroller or other serial source device. The lower waveform shows the same waveform converted to RS232C levels. An RS232C is usually used to transmit serial data between devices such as personal computers, terminals, or modems. The voltage levels of the RS232C are used to assure error-free transmission over greater distances than would be possible with TTL levels.

As shown in Figure 4–11, each byte is preceded by a start bit and followed by one (or sometimes two) stop bit(s). The start and stop bits are used to synchronize the serial receivers. The data byte is always transmitted least-significant-bit first. For error checking it is possible to include a parity bit as well, just prior to the stop bit. The bits are transmitted at specific time intervals determined by the **baud rate** of the serial signal. The baud rate is the reciprocal of the time to send 1 bit. Error-free serial communication requires that

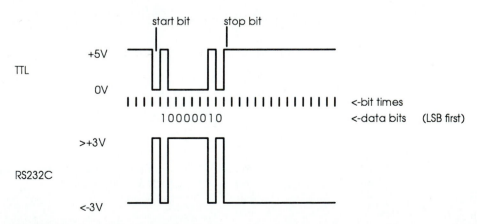

FIGURE 4–11   Serial waveforms.

the baud rate, number of data bits, number of stop bits, and presence or absence of a parity bit be the same at the transmitter and at the receiver.

The 8051 family provides one channel (both transmit and receive) of serial communication. The transmit data (TXD) and receive data (RXD) pins are among the alternate functions on port 3. The serial signals provided on these pins are TTL signal levels and must be boosted (and inverted) through the use of a suitable driver and receiver to comply with RS232 standards for serial communications with other devices. Figure 4–12 shows the pulse measurement system of Figure 4–6 with the serial port added to allow serial communication of the pulse-width measurement results. The program transmits the resulting count bytes in hex via the serial line. If a terminal display device is connected to the serial output, the bytes will be displayed in normal hex format.

Using the Serial Port

The serial port in the 8051 family of microcontrollers is capable of supporting a variety of serial communication protocols. Included are multiprocessor communications and other special modes, which are covered in Chapter 6. This section concentrates on the more usual, asynchronous communications. All modes are controlled through SCON, the Serial CONtrol register. The details of the SCON are shown in Figure 4–13.

The SCON controls the modes through bits SM0 and SM1. The usual mode is mode 1, the variable baud rate mode used for asynchronous serial communication. In this mode timer 1 is used to provide the baud rate clock for the serial port.

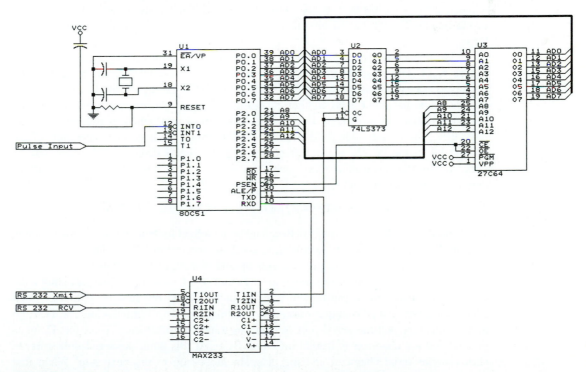

FIGURE 4–12 Pulse measurement system with serial communication.

FIGURE 4–13 SCON bit
definitions.

In addition to SM0 and SM1, SCON contains SM2, a bit that controls the multiprocessor communication mode. This mode is discussed in Chapter 6.

The REN bit is set to enable the serial receiver, and the TB8 and RB8 bits are the ninth bits to be transmitted or received in mode 2 but are unused in mode 1. TI and RI are the transmit and receive interrupt bits. They indicate the transmission and the reception, respectively, of a serial character. These two bits can be polled by the program to determine whether serial data has been received or sent in a similar manner to polling the TFx bit in the timers. The TI and RI bits may also function as interrupts as described in Chapter 6.

The assembly-language software for the pulse measurement system is shown in Figure 4–14. The program adds the necessary steps to cause the counter contents to be displayed in hex on a serial terminal attached to the 8051 serial port. Mode 1 of the serial port requires that timer 1 be configured in mode 2, 8-bit auto-reload mode. Each time the timer reloads, it provides a clock pulse to the serial port, which is used as the baud rate clock. The reload value for the port, then, determines the baud rate. The value of the SMOD bit in the PCON, the power control register, helps determine the baud rate as indicated by the formula. Usually SMOD is left at 0, the reset state. The formula to determine the correct baud rate is

$$\text{Baud rate} = (2^{\text{smod}}/32) * (\text{osc freq}/(12 * (256 - \text{TH1})))$$

The formula must be solved for TH1 to calculate the reload for baud rates. For the example shown, the reload rate is 0xfd, resulting in a calculation of 9600 baud. The program also shows some useful subroutines for conversion and display of hex numbers.

The 'sero:' section of the program in Figure 4–14 (starting at line 37) shows the correct way to use the serial port to transmit data. The TI bit must be initialized high (line 7) to allow the sero output routine to function. The sero routine waits for TI to go high, indicating that the serial port is ready to transmit a character. Then the TI bit is cleared and the character is loaded into the SBUF. At this point the serial port starts to shift out the serial character and the program moves on to the next step. When that character is completely transmitted, the TI is automatically set so that the program can

```
 1 pulse    equ    INT0
 2
 3          org    2000h
 4 init:    mov    tmod,#29h    ;gate=1,mode 1
 5          mov    th1,#0fdh    ;9600 baud
 6          mov    tcon,#00h    ;clear all bits
 7          mov    scon,#42h    ;8-bit async
 8          setb   tr1          ;timer on
 9 loop:    jb     pulse,loop   ;wait for pulse low
10          clr    tf0          ;clear timer flag
11          setb   tr0          ;timer 0 on
12          mov    th0,#00      ;clear counters
13          mov    tl0,#00
14 waithi:  jnb    pulse,waithi ;wait for pulse high
15 waitpl:  jb     pulse,waitpl ;wait for pulse done
16          jb     tf0,loop     ;jump if rollover
17          mov    a,th0        ;get msb of count
18          acall  disbyt       ;transmit msb of count
19          mov    a,tl0        ;get lsb of count
20          acall  disbyt       ;transmit msb of count
21          mov    a,','        ;transmit a comma
22          acall  sero         ;to separate entries
23          sjmp   loop         ;go back for next pulse
24
25 disbyt:  mov    r7,a         ;display a hex byte in A
26          swap   a            ;exchange nybbles
27          call   disnyb       ;display MSnybble
28          mov    a,r7         ;get lower nybble
29          call   disnyb       ;display LSnybble
30          ret
31
32 disnyb:  anl    a,#0fh       ;display a nybble
33          add    a,#90h       ;adjust for ASCII
34          da     a            ;by adding 144,
35          addc   a,#40h       ;adjusting and adding
36          da     a            ;64
37 sero:    jnb    ti,sero      ;ready?
38          clr    ti           ;clear for next time
39          mov    sbuf,a       ;send byte
40          ret
41          end
```

FIGURE 4–14 Pulse measurement system software.

tell whether the serial port is ready for the next transmission. The TI therefore allows the processor to be busy doing other things while the serial port is sending the data (the TI is not used in this manner in the sample program). The processor need only check the TI occasionally to see if the serial port needs attention.

Downloaders

As a further example of serial communication, the following software is used. As described in Chapter 3, assemblers produce assembled code in machine language for the microcontroller. This code usually takes the form of an INTEL-format hex file. The INTEL hex file is designed to be used by loading it into an EPROM to be executed by the microprocessor or to be used by downloading it into a development system with a suitable monitor program. A monitor program is a program that runs in the embedded microcontroller and that allows other microcontroller programs to be loaded and run. The program shown in Figure 4–15 is a simple downloader. It can use the INTEL hex-format files and load them into the memory of the microcontroller for execution. This particular program expects the assembly language to be ORGed at 0x2000 and automatically jumps to that location once

```
 1              org     3000h
 2
 3 init:   mov     scon,#50h;8 bin UART, RCV enabled
 4         mov     tmod,#20h;set timer 1 mode 1
 5         mov     tcon,#0   ;nothing running
 6         mov     th1,#0fdh;reload value
 7         setb    tr1        ;start timer 1
 8
 9 inp:    call    serin     ;get character
10         cjne    a,#3ah,inp;wait for : (3ah)
11         call    ghd       ;get a byte
12         mov     b,a       ;number of bytes
13         call    ghd
14         mov     dph,a     ;msb of addr
15         call    ghd
16         mov     dpl,a     ;lsb of addr
17         call    ghd       ;record type
18         jz      getlin    ;if type =1, end
19         call    ghd
20         ljmp    2000h     ;jump to run program
21 getlin: call    ghd       ;get data byte
22         movx    @dptr,a   ;store in memory
23         inc     dptr      ;next address
24         djnz    b,getlin  ;do until no data
25         call    ghd       ;blow off checksum
26         jmp     inp
27
28 ghd:    call    getnyb    ;get hex digit serially
29         swap    a         ;exchange nybbles
30         mov     r7,a      ;save MSnybble
31         call    getnyb    ;get LSnybble
32         orl     a,r7      ;combine nybbles and return
33         ret
34
35 getnyb: call    serin     ;get nybble from crt
36         jnb     acc.6,getret;jump if numeric
37         clr     acc.5     ;make upper case
38         add     a,#9      ;adjust for ASCII
39 getret: anl     a,#0fh    ;mask upper nybble
40         ret
41
42 serin:  jnb     ri,serin;ready?
43         clr     ri        ;clear for next time
44         mov     a,sbuf    ;get byte
45         ret               ;return with character
46         end
```

FIGURE 4–15 Assembly-language downloader.

the program is loaded. The program thus provides a working downloader/monitor for INTEL-format hex files.

The downloader may be used in the development process as discussed in Chapter 3. This downloader expects that INTEL-formatted hex files are input via the serial port.

In order to see the operation of the downloader, it is necessary to understand the format of INTEL hex files. These files are ASCII-coded representations of executable files. Since they are ASCII formatted, they can be transferred by normal serial communications. The catch is that the downloader must re-create the executable file and place it into the proper memory locations. In this case the downloader loads the executable file and then automatically executes the program beginning at 0x2000. Assuming that the program being downloaded starts at 0x2000, the program can be downloaded and run in one operation. Intel hex format is shown in Figure 4–16.

The INTEL hex files do not contain spaces, but Figure 4–16 has been altered to include the column labels and the spaces for clarity. Each pair of numbers is read by the downloader and converted to a hex byte.

The column labeled ''cc'' is the data byte count, which tells the downloader how many data bytes are included in this line of code. The word in column ''aaaa'' contains the address into which the first byte of data in the line must be loaded. The ''tt'' column contains a type-code byte. The two possible types are 00 (data) and 01 (the end-of-data line). If the downloader discovers a type code of 0, it knows that the line contains cc bytes of data, which need to be placed in memory beginning at aaaa (the specified address). The data bytes that follow the typecode are placed into successive memory locations in the order in which they appear in the line of hex code. A type code of 1 indicates that the line is the last line of the file and the downloading should cease.

The last byte in each line (separated from the data bytes by a space) is the check sum for the line. The check sum is an error-checking device. The check sum is calculated by figuring the 2s complement of the sum of the bytes in the line. The receiving computer can calculate the check sum for each line of data received and then compare it to the check sum in the data line. If the two do not agree, then a transmission error has occurred and the data are faulty. Using the second line of Figure 4–16 as an example, the check sum is calculated as follows:

1. Add the bytes in the line, discarding any carries.

$$0x02 + 0x20 + 0x2c + 0x00 + 0xe5 + 0x22 = 0x55$$

Note: The sum is really 0x155, but the 1 is a carry and is discarded.

2. Take the 1s complement of 0x55.

$$1s \text{ complement of } 0x55 = 0xaa$$

3. Add 1 to get the 2s complement.

$$0xaa + 0x1 = 0xab$$

FIGURE 4–16 INTEL hex format.

```
:cc aaaa tt data
:10 201C 00 30B2FD20B2FD208DED858A08858C0980 BB
:02 202C 00 E522 AB
:00 0000 01 FF
```

Note that the result, 0xab, agrees with the check sum at the end of the second line in Figure 4–16.

The downloader program shown in Figure 4–15 first initializes the timer and serial ports as explained previously. Lines 9 and 10 wait for a ":" to denote the beginning of a line of code. After receiving the ":", the program reads the next two bytes and assembles them into the single data byte that indicates the count of data bytes on the line. Then the address word and type-code byte are read in a similar manner and the address is stored in the data pointer. The *getlin* routine gets the line of code (all the data bytes) and places them into memory in sequential locations.

The *ghd* subroutine gets the two characters of each byte and assembles them into a hex byte that is then returned to the main program. The *serin* subroutine demonstrates the method of polling RI until a serial character is received. Note that the character received is found in the SBUF after the RI goes high. Study of the downloader will clarify the use of the serial port, the timer as a baud rate generator, and the use of a downloader for program development.

4–4   SUMMARY

The 8051 microcontroller contains a number of built-in peripherals. These include parallel ports to transfer bit-size or byte-wide parallel data into and out of the microcontroller. The 8051 family also includes two counter/timer units, which may be used to measure pulse widths or frequencies, or to provide variable-frequency signals as outputs, or which may be used to provide accurate time delays. The serial ports and serial communication are commonly used to communicate with or to control members of the 8051 family.

4–5   EXERCISES

1. Write a parallel data transfer program using strobe-and-acknowledge handshaking. The strobe pulse is to a positive-going pulse and the acknowledge will indicate ready on the negative-going edge. Use the hardware setup of Figure 4–2.
2. Write the necessary code lines to initialize timer 1 to be externally clocked in mode 0.
3. Recalculate the reload factor to provide a 1-ms delay using the delay routine of Figure 4–9.
4. Recalculate the reload number for line 5 of Figure 4–14 to allow communication at 2400 baud.
5. Draw the waveform seen on the serial transmit pin of an 8051 transmitting 0x5a as a data byte. Identify the start bit, the stop bit, and the data bits. Use 8 data bits and 1 stop bit, and do not include a parity bit.
6. Draw the wave form from Exercise 5 using RS232C levels.

7. If you were to use an 8051 processor with a 10-MHz crystal to measure a pulse width as shown in this chapter, what would the actual pulse width be if the count after the pulse were to be 0x4e5c?

8. Using the following line of INTEL-format hex code, identify the number of data bytes and list them. Also identify the address at which each byte would be placed and recalculate the check sum to verify the integrity of the data.

:0730100006e3a1887f8a326c

CHAPTER 5

External Peripherals

OVERVIEW

This chapter deals with external devices that are commonly used with the 8051 family of microcontrollers. Some of these devices can either be interfaced via the parallel ports or memory mapped into the system as on-bus devices (refer to Chapter 2). The examples in this chapter deal with the on-bus case, since that is the more common and the more stringent. Any of the on-bus devices can be interfaced using a parallel port by providing all the same signals via software through the port.

Figure 5–1 shows an 80C31-based system that provides the capability to input and output analog signals. Also included are an LCD display for visual output and a keypad for control input. This system is the basis for the examples in much of this chapter.

5–1   ANALOG-TO-DIGITAL AND DIGITAL-TO-ANALOG CONVERTERS

The world outside the microcontroller is, in general, analog in nature. Analog-to-digital converters (ADCs) and digital-to-analog converters (DACs) provide the means whereby microcontrollers can interact with these analog signals. ADCs input an analog voltage and provide a digital measurement of the instantaneous voltage; DACs output an analog voltage based on a digital value. Figure 5–1 shows an ADC and a DAC in a configuration appropriate for an analog control system. This system could be used for temperature control of an oven or incubator, for instance, by using the ADC to measure the temperature and the DAC to control the heater. The system is useful for controlling anything that can be measured and controlled via analog signals.

The DAC shown is an AD558 Dacport, manufactured by Analog Devices. The DAC provides 0–10 VDC output proportional to the digital word input on DB0 through DB7. The digital data are latched into the DAC when both the $\overline{CE}$ and $\overline{CS}$ signals are low simultaneously. Allowing for propagation time, the voltage corresponding to the data appears on the output as soon as the digital data byte is latched into the DAC. In this example the DAC's $\overline{CS}$ control line is tied to the 74HC138 memory decoder output that

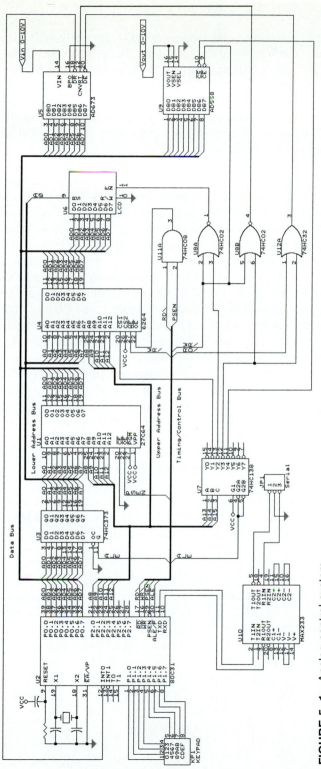

FIGURE 5–1 Analog control system.

is enabled by addresses in the range of 0x8000 through 0x9FFF. The DAC's $\overline{\text{CE}}$ control line is tied to the $\overline{\text{WR}}$ line of the control bus. Referring to the memory-write cycle shown in Figure 2–7, the only time these two lines can be low simultaneously is when data are written to an address in the range of 0x8000 through 09fff. Thus any data written to addresses in this range will be latched into the DAC and will determine the analog output voltage. Typically, a programmer uses a single address such as 0x8000 to refer to the ADC or DAC device. It is important to remember, however, that data written to any of the addresses in the device's range will cause the same result as an access to the single address.

The ADC shown is interfaced to the bus in a similar manner. The ADC is a type AD673, also manufactured by Analog Devices. ADCs are not instantaneous devices. There is a finite time (often 100 μs or more) from the time the conversion is started until valid data are available. This time is known as the **conversion time.** As a result, some handshaking is required to interface with the relatively slow device, the ADC. The microcontroller sends a **convert pulse** to the ADC to start the conversion, and the ADC signals the completion of the conversion with the data ready line. The ADC requires a positive-going pulse to be applied to the CNVRT pin to start a conversion. Following the convert pulse, the data ready ($\overline{\text{DR}}$) pin goes to a logic 1 (the ''busy'' state) and is held there during the conversion. When the conversion is complete and the data are valid and available, the data ready pin ($\overline{\text{DR}}$) is returned low. At this point the ADC data are valid and the microprocessor can read the data.

The convert pulse is supplied by writing data to any address 0x6000 through 0x7fff. The WR\ control line and the Y3 output are NORed together to provide the convert pulse when data are written to any of these addresses. The same Y3 output from the 74HC138 memory decoder and the $\overline{\text{RD}}$ control line are ORed together to allow the microprocessor to read the ADC data by reading any address falling in the same range. Writing to any of the ADC addresses, then, starts the conversion. Monitoring the $\overline{\text{DR}}$ line from the ADC allows the microprocessor to wait for the slower ADC and then to read the data from the same addresses when the conversion is complete. Continuously checking to see if an event has occurred (i.e., monitoring the $\overline{\text{DR}}$ line) is referred to as **polling.**

The digital and analog values associated with ADCs and DACs may be calculated using the following simple ratio formula:

$$\frac{V}{V_{\text{FS}}} = \frac{\text{digital value}}{2^n - 1}$$

where V is the instantaneous voltage into the ADC or out of the DAC, V_{FS} is the full-scale voltage of the ADC or DAC, the digital value is the binary value applied to the DAC or the value read from the ADC, and n is the number of data bits transferred from or to the microprocessor. Assume that the ADC in the example system has 2.13 VDC applied to its input. In that case the ratio formula is

$$\frac{2.13}{10.0} = \frac{X}{2^8 - 1}$$

$$X = 255 * \frac{2.13}{10.0}$$

$$X = 54.32_{10} = 36_{16} = 00110110_2$$

In reality, only integer numbers can be input to a DAC or output from an ADC. In this example the processor would read 54 (actually, the processor would read 0x36 . . . 54 expressed in hex). The integer nature of DACs and ADCs is caused by the binary nature of the numbers input to a DAC or output from an ADC. In other words, a DAC can only output voltage in discrete steps (± 1 bit at the digital interface), and an ADC can only read voltage to within 1 bit at the digital interface. This feature of ADCs and DACs is called **resolution** and is calculated by

$$\text{Resolution} = \frac{V_{FS}}{2^n - 1}$$

It is largely the resolution that limits the accuracy of the voltage output from a DAC or the measurement ability of an ADC. The only ways to improve resolution are to reduce the full-scale voltage of the device or increase the number of bits in the digital interface.

Figures 5–2 and 5–3 show examples of programs that use the ADC and DAC in the example system. The two programs do exactly the same thing. They first output 54_{10} to the DAC and then they read the ADC by first pulsing the ADC convert line, then waiting for the $\overline{DR}$ line to indicate that the data are ready, and finally reading the ADC data. Note that the programmer has chosen to assign a single address to the ADC and DAC even though they respond to a whole range of addresses. As is typical, the address used is the lowest address in the range. Both programs end with an infinite loop for test purposes.

5–2 LIQUID-CRYSTAL DISPLAYS

Figure 5–1 demonstrates the use of a typical liquid-crystal display (LCD) as an on-bus peripheral. An LCD is an "intelligent" display in that it contains integrated electronics. The microprocessor need only provide several initialization bytes to set the display for

FIGURE 5–2 Assembly-language ADC/DAC program

```
;Program to write DAC and read ADC.
DAC        equ  8000h      ;DAC address
ADC        equ  6000H      ;ADC address
           org  0000h

strt:      sjmp main ;jump around subroutine

adrd:      mov  dptr,#ADC
           movx @dptr,a    ;make convert pulse
wate:      jb   INT0,wate;wait for DR\ low
           movx a,@dptr    ;read ADC
           ret

main:      mov  a,#54      ;load a with 54
           mov  dptr,#DAC
           movx @dptr,a    ;load DAC with 54
           acall     adrd ;read ADC
stay:      sjmp stay ;wait forever
           end
```

FIGURE 5–3 C-language ADC/DAC program.

```
#include <c:\c51\reg52.h>
#include <c:\c51\absacc.h>
#define DAC XBYTE[0x8000]   /*DAC in/out*/
#define ADC XBYTE[0x6000]   /*ADC input*/

unsigned char adcrd()
    {
    ADC = 00;   /*make convert pulse*/
    while (INT0==1);  /*wait for DR\ low*/
    return ADC;  /*read ADC*/
    }

main()
    {
    unsigned char x;
    DAC = 54;   /*output 54 to DAC*/
    x = adcrd();   /*read ADC*/
    while(1);   /*meaningless wait loop*/
    }
```

an operating mode to fit the project, then supply ASCII data for those characters to be displayed. The display has one register into which commands are sent, and one register into which data to be displayed are sent. The two registers are differentiated by a single control line on the LCD.

The interface to the LCD consists of eight data lines (d0–d7) and control lines [Enable (E), Register Select (RS), and Read/Write (R/W)]. The data lines are used to transfer both commands (clear, home, cursor positioning, etc.) and data (characters to be displayed). The LCD will treat the incoming bytes as commands when RS is low and as data to be displayed when RS is high. In the example system, RS is connected to A0, so writing to an even address will be treated as a command by the LCD while writing to an odd address will be treated as data.

The enable pulse on the LCD shown is a positive-going pulse that is synchronous with and the same length as $\overline{WR}$ or $\overline{RD}$ depending on whether the LCD is being written to or read. It is sometimes convenient to be able to read the currently displayed information in systems with little or no memory or to be able to read the LCD status register for handshaking purposes. In the system of Figure 5–1, it is impossible to read the data or status register since R/$\overline{W}$ is tied low. The enable pulse in the example system is provided by NORing $\overline{WR}$ and one chip select from the address decoder. In this case the chip select is for the address range 0x4000 to 0x5fff. Thus a byte written to any even address within this range will be treated as a command by the LCD, and a byte written to any odd address within this range will be treated as data to be displayed. Normally the data to be displayed is ASCII-coded data (see Appendix B). If the display is to be read, the R/W line would be connected to the system $\overline{WR}$ so that the R/W would be high when a ''read'' occurs, or low for a ''write.'' It would also be necessary to add combinational logic such that the enable pulse occurs when either $\overline{WR}$ or $\overline{RD}$ occurs in conjunction with the correct chip select.

LCDs usually require some initialization commands. These are described in the data sheets for the particular display used. The subroutines or functions usually used to send characters or commands to the LCD are shown in Figures 5–4 and 5–5. These two figures

```
 1        LCDCMD   equ      4000h    ;LCD command address
 2        LCDDATA  equ      4001h    ;LCD data address
 3
 4                 org      0000h
 5        start:   ljmp     init     ;jump to main program
 6
 7        wrdata:  mov      dptr,#LCDDATA
 8                 movx     @dptr,a ;write data to LCD
 9                 ret
10        wrcmd:   mov      dptr,#LCDCMD
11                 movx     @dptr,a ;write LCD command
12                 ret
13        init:    ;----    >>>initialize LCD here<<<
14                 ;----
15                 ;----
16                 mov      a,#34h   ;output 34H as an LCD command
17                 lcall    wrcmd
18                 ;----
19                 ;----
20                 ;----
21                 mov      a,#57h   ;output 57h as data to LCD
22                 lcall    wrdata
23                 ;----
24                 ;----
25                 end
```

FIGURE 5-4   Assembly-language LCD subroutines.

```
 1   #include <c:\c51\reg52.h>
 2   #include <c:\c51\absacc.h>
 3   #define LCDDATA XBYTE[0x4001]  /*LCD command address*/
 4   #define LCDCMD XBYTE[0x6000]   /*LCD data address*/
 5
 6   void wrlcddata (unsigned char ch)
 7     {
 8     LCDDATA = ch; /*write character to LCD*/
 9     }
10   void wrlcdcmd (unsigned char cmd)
11             {
12     LCDCMD = cmd; /*write lcd command*/
13     }
14
15   main()
16     {
17     /* >>>initialize LCD here<<< */
18     wrlcdcmd(0x34);   /*write 34h as an LCD command*/
19     wrlcddata(0x57);  /*write 56h as data to the LCD*/
20     }
```

FIGURE 5-5   C-language LCD functions.

show examples of subroutines and functions that could be used with a typical LCD display connected as shown in the example system. These subroutines do not include any delays or handshaking, which may be required by some LCD displays. For example, commands such as *clear* usually require more time than would be allowed if the microcontroller outputs data as fast as it can. This is a typical use of handshaking. In this case handshaking is accomplished by using the status word read from the LCD. This status word will have a bit that shows when the LCD is ready for more data. If the option to read the LCD status is not provided, as in Figure 5–1, time delays must be provided to allow the LCD to complete its commands. The data sheets for the LCD being used will provide more details. The LCD could also be controlled via a parallel port by connecting all the LCD data and control lines to the port. Software would then be needed to provide all the control signals and data for the LCD.

5–3   KEYPADS

Keypads (or individual switches wired as if they were keypads) are often used as a primary input device for embedded microcontrollers. The keypads actually consist of a number of switches (the keypad shown in Figure 5–1 has 16) connected in a row/column arrangement as shown in Figure 5–6.

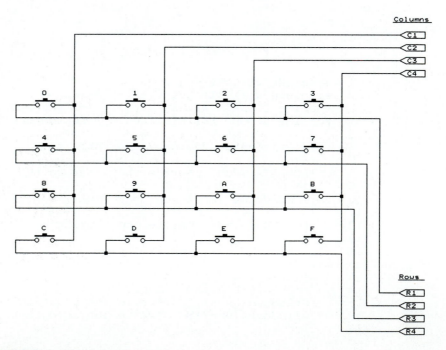

FIGURE 5–6 Hex keypad.

In order for the microcontroller to scan the keypad, it drives (outputs) a nybble to force one (only one) of the columns low and then reads the rows to see if any buttons in that column have been pressed. The rows are pulled up by the internal weak pull-ups in the 8051 family ports. Consequently, as long as no buttons are pressed, the microcontroller sees a logic high on each of the pins attached to the keypad rows. The nybble driven onto the columns always contains only a single 0. The only way the microcontroller can find a 0 on any row pin is for a keypad button to be pressed that connects the column set to 0 to a row. The controller knows which column is at a 0 level and which row reads 0, allowing it to determine which key is pressed.

Figures 5–7 and 5–8 show programs to scan the keypad. Lines 5, 6, and 7 of the assembly-language program check to see that all keys are released before starting the scan. Similarly, lines 50 and 51 in the C program wait for the keys to be released before allowing a new scan. This is accomplished by setting all the columns to 0 and waiting for all the rows to be high. As long as any keys are pressed, one or more rows will be low. The programs shown both scan the keypad by setting one of the column lines low (starting with column 0) and then looking for any of the row lines to be low. If none is found to be low (no buttons are pressed), then the bit connected to column 0 is returned high and the bit connected to column 1 is set low, the rows are rechecked, and so on. If a row is found to be at 0 (meaning that a button has been pressed), the scan routine stops and a routine is entered that converts the keybutton row/column code to the number of the button pressed.

Both programs contain a dummy print routine. This routine could be replaced with the LCD driver subroutine or function shown in Figure 5–4 or 5–5. The dummy display routine could also be replaced by the seven-segment scanner routine discussed later (which would eliminate the need to convert the keystroke to ASCII), or it could be replaced by a routine to print the number via a display attached to the serial port.

The two programs differ in the manner in which they handle the scanning function. The assembly-code routine calls the scanning routine and then waits for a keypress to occur. The microcontroller is thus held up until a keypress occurs. The C program uses a scanning routine that returns 0xff if it completes a scan and no keypress has occurred. This way the program can scan the keypad and then do other tasks before again scanning the keypad. The advantage to the scan-until-pressed method is that the microcontroller is always ready for a keypress to occur and does not miss any. The disadvantage, of course, is that the microcontroller is busy scanning and waiting for a keypress and cannot do anything else. The scan-and-return method allows the microcontroller to do other tasks but has the disadvantage that it may miss a keypress because it is busy when the press occurs. A better method of scanning using timer interrupts is presented in Chapter 6.

The keypad may also be scanned by a keypad decoder IC, which then can be read by the microcontroller. The decoder, if used, is usually an on-bus peripheral and frees up the microcontroller to do other tasks. Figure 5–9 shows a decoder to interface between the keypad of Figure 5–6 and the microcontroller bus. The data bus is connected to the decoder data pins, and the $\overline{CS}$ (from a 74LS138 decoder) and $\overline{RD}$ are ORed together to control the output enable ($\overline{OE}$) of the keypad decoder. This arrangement allows the output of the keypad decoder to be driven onto the data bus when $\overline{RD}$ is low and the proper address is output (i.e., the microcontroller is reading the decoder).

```
 1  ; Keypad scanning program.
 2          org      2000h
 3  start:  ljmp     init     ;jump to main program
 4
 5  scan:   mov      P1,#0f0h;check for buttons pressed
 6          mov      a,P1      ;by observing P1
 7          cjne     a,#0f0h,scan
 8  scanner:mov      a,#0feh  ;beginning pattern
 9  lup:    mov      r0,a      ;save output pattern
10          mov      P1,a      ;output pattern
11          mov      a,P1      ;read port
12          mov      r1,a      ;save keyread
13          orl      a,#0fh   ;set drive bits high
14          cjne     a,#0ffh,cnvrt ;jump if key pressed
15          mov      a,r0      ;recover drive
16          rl       a         ;rotate drive bit left
17          cjne     a,#0efh,lup ;jump to scan next col
18          sjmp     scanner  ;start a new scan
19
20  cnvrt:  mov      a,r1      ;recover keyread
21          mov      r3,#0     ;clear table counter
22  clup:   jnb      acc.0,cnvrt2;done with major count
23          rr       a         ;rotate value
24          mov      r2,a      ;save rotated value
25          mov      a,r3      ;incr counter
26          add      a,#4      ;add 4 per column
27          mov      r3,a      ;save count
28          mov      a,r2      ;recover rotating value
29          sjmp     clup
30  cnvrt2: mov      a,r1      ;recover keyread
31          swap     a         ;exchange nybbles to get rows
32  clup2:  jnb      acc.0,xlat;jump to translate reading
33          rr       a         ;rotate to find zero
34          inc      r3        ;bump counter
35          sjmp     clup2     ;jump to check next bit
36  xlat:   mov      a,r3      ;get count
37          mov      dptr,#keytab ;point to translate table
38          movc     a,@a+dptr ;get translated character
39          ret
40
41  DSPLY:  ret                ;dummy display subr.
42
43  init:   acall    scan      ;get keystroke
44          mov      r0,a      ;save the character
45          clr      c         ;clear carry for subtraction
46          subb     a,#0ah    ;check for > 10
47          jnc      letter    ;jump if > 10
48          mov      a,r0      ;recover character
49          orl      a,#30h    ;make number ASCII
50          sjmp     dply      ;jump around
51  letter: mov      a,r0      ;recover character
52          add      a,#55     ;adjust for ASCII
53  dply:   lcall    DSPLY     ;display it
54          sjmp     init      ;do it again
```

FIGURE 5-7   Assembly-language keypad scanner.

```
1    #define KEYPAD P1
2    #include <c:\c51\reg52.h>
3    #include <c:\c51\absacc.h>
4
5    void DSPLY(unsigned char hexnum) {} /* dummy*/
6
7    unsigned char scan(void)
8        {
9        unsigned char scandrive = 0xfe; /*scanner drive*/
10       unsigned char count = 0;/*counter for conversion*/
11       unsigned char key, majorkey, minorkey;
12       unsigned char keytab[] = {0,4,8,0xc,1,5,9,0xd,2,6,
                 0xa,0xe,3,7,0xb,0xf};
13       key = 0xf0; /*preset key*/
14       while ((scandrive != 0xef)&&((key & 0XF0)==0XF0))
15           {
16           KEYPAD = scandrive; /*output drive*/
17           key = KEYPAD; /*read keypad*/
18           scandrive=(scandrive*2)+1;/*shift drive left*/
19           }
20       if (key == 0xf7) return 0xff; /*key not pressed*/
21       else
22           {
23           majorkey = key; /*get key and drive code*/
24           while ((majorkey & 0x01) != 0)
25               {
26               count = count + 4; /*increment major count*/
27               majorkey=(majorkey>>1);/*shift right 1 bit*/
28               }
29           minorkey=(key>>4);/*get minor key and drive*/
30           while ((minorkey & 0x01) != 0)
31               {
32               count++; /*increment minor count*/
33               minorkey = (minorkey >> 1); /*shift right*/
34               }
35           return keytab[count]; /*translate key press*/
36           }
37       }
38
39   main()
40       {
41       unsigned char keypress;/*variable for keypress*/
42       while (1) /*do forever*/
43           {
44           keypress = scan(); /*get keypress info*/
45           if (keypress != 0xff) /*key pressed is new*/
46               {
47               if(keypress<0x0a)keypress=(keypress|0x30);
                         /*make numeric characters ASCII*/
48               else keypress = keypress + 55;
                         /*make alpha characters ASCII*/
49               DSPLY(keypress); /*display character*/
50               KEYPAD = 0xf0; /*hold for key release*/
51               while (KEYPAD != 0xf0);
52               }
53           }
54       }
```

FIGURE 5–8 C-language keypad scanner.

FIGURE 5–9 Keypad decoder.

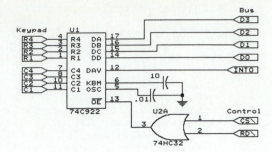

Use of this decoder requires that the microcontroller know when a key is pressed. The Data AVailable (DAV) pin on the decoder chip is set to a logic high when a key is pressed. The microcontroller can poll the DAV to detect a keypress. The microcontroller must poll this pin relatively often (within 100 milliseconds) to avoid missing keypresses. The 100ms time limit is not limiting and the microcontroller can accomplish many other tasks while polling the DAV pin.

The other method to detect a keypress is to use the DAV as an interrupt (see Chapter 6). An interrupt frees the microcontroller to complete other tasks until the keypress occurs.

5–4   SEVEN SEGMENT LED DISPLAYS

In many embedded controllers it is important to have a very visible display. In these cases an LED seven-segment display is often used. The displays can be driven in several ways, although they are most often driven via a parallel port. The simplest, shown in Figure 5–10, has the microcontroller directly driving the displays via appropriate buffers. This circuit requires that the microcontroller determine the appropriate code to output to the displays in order to show numbers and a few letters. A disadvantage to this circuit is that it requires one 8-bit port per digit displayed.

In the circuit shown in Figure 5–10, a logic 0 will cause the segment of the display to illuminate. The segments are designated by the letters *a* through *g:*

FIGURE 5-10 Directly
driven seven-segment display.

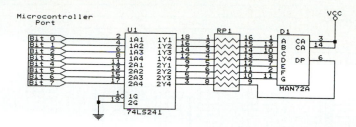

The segments are illuminated by applying the codes shown in Figure 5-11 via the parallel port.

Figure 5-12 shows a circuit similar to Figure 5-10 except that a decoder/driver has replaced the buffer. The 7447 decoder/driver takes care of the code conversion, requiring only the BCD equivalent of the digit to produce an appropriate display. Programs using this circuit need only output the BCD code for each digit to be displayed.

The circuit of Figure 5-12 requires only 4 bits of a parallel port to work (plus 1 bit for the decimal point, if used). With a bit of care in programming, two digits can be run from a single 8-bit port. For displays of more digits it is normal to use a scanned display as shown in Figure 5-13.

The circuit shown in Figure 5-13 allows displaying up to four digits from one 8-bit port (actually, 16 digits could be displayed with additional logic). It requires that the

FIGURE 5-11 Seven-
segment drive codes.

Digit	G	F	E	D	C	B	A	Hex
0	1	0	0	0	0	0	0	40
1	1	1	1	1	0	0	1	79
2	0	1	0	0	1	0	0	24
3	0	1	1	0	0	0	0	30
4	0	0	1	0	0	0	1	11
5	0	0	1	0	0	1	0	12
6	0	0	0	0	0	1	0	02
7	1	1	1	1	0	0	0	78
8	0	0	0	0	0	0	0	00
9	0	0	1	1	0	0	0	18

FIGURE 5-12 Decoder-
driven seven-segment display.

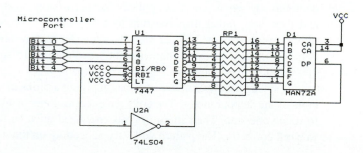

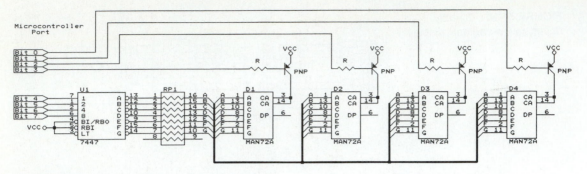

FIGURE 5–13 Scanned seven-segment display.

microcontroller output the data to be displayed for the first digit and activate that digit by outputting a low to the base of the transistor switch and delaying for a short time. Then the microcontroller raises the base of the switching transistor, shutting off current to the digit. It then outputs the data to the next digit and turns on its current switch. This process repeats until all digits have been lighted and then repeats. As long as the scanning occurs at a rate faster than the human eye can follow (approximately 42 Hz), the display will appear to be consistently on.

The current will flow during only one-fourth of the available time, making the *average* current one-fourth of the on-time current. The display will therefore appear dim unless the resistor is reduced to bring the average current up to the specification value for the display digit. At this point the resistor will be such that, if the scanning stops with a digit energized, four times the maximum current will flow in the digit, possibly burning it out. Because of the need to provide continuous scanning, the display is best handled through more advanced techniques such as timer interrupts. An example of such a program is given in Chapter 6.

5–5   STEPPER MOTORS

Stepper motors are often used in conjunction with microcontrollers to provide precisely controlled motive power. Stepper motors are devices that rotate a precise number of degrees for each "step" applied, as opposed to regular motors, which simply rotate continuously when power is applied. Stepper motors rotate the correct number of steps and then stop, rather than coasting to a stop like DC or AC motors. Typically, stepper motors rotate 15° or 7.5° per step. Usually the motors are specified by the number of complete steps it takes to complete a 360° revolution (a 15°-per-step motor would complete 1 revolution in 24 steps—a "24-step" motor).

Driving a stepper motor involves applying a series of voltages to the four (typically) coils of the stepper motor. The coils are energized one or two at a time to cause the motor to rotate one step. The pattern of coils energized must be followed exactly for the motor to work correctly. The pattern will vary depending on the mode used with the motor. The

FIGURE 5–14 Direct-drive stepper motor.

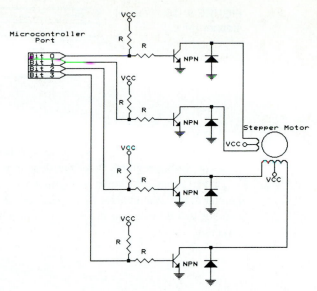

The diodes shown are transient protection diodes

normal mode for low-torque applications is the half-step mode, in which a 24-step motor will actually take 48 steps to complete a revolution. A direct-drive interface to drive a stepper motor through a parallel port is shown in Figure 5–14.

The interface shown in Figure 5–14 requires that the microcontroller output the drive pattern to make the motor rotate. A half-step drive pattern for the stepper motor shown in Figure 5–14 is shown in Figure 5–15.

For higher-torque applications the normal step sequence is used. This sequence is shown in Figure 5–16. In order to control the stepper motor, the microcontroller must output the values shown in the figure *in the sequence shown*. Figures 5–15 and 5–16 are circular in that after the last step, the next output must be the first step. The values may be output in the order shown to rotate the motor one direction or in reverse order to rotate in the reverse direction. It is essential that the order be preserved even if the motor is stopped for a while. The next step to restart the motor must be the next sequential step following the last step used. The mechanical inertia of the motor will require a short delay (usually 5 to 15 ms) between each step to avoid the motor missing steps.

FIGURE 5–15 Half-step drive sequence.

Step	Bit 3	Bit 2	Bit 1	Bit 0
1	1	0	1	0
2	1	0	0	0
3	1	0	0	1
4	0	0	0	1
5	0	1	0	1
6	0	1	0	0
7	0	1	1	0
8	0	0	1	0

FIGURE 5–16 Normal stepper drive.

Step	Bit 3	Bit 2	Bit 1	Bit 0
1	1	0	1	0
2	1	0	0	1
3	0	1	0	1
4	0	1	1	0

The programs shown in Figures 5–17 and 5–18 will cause the motor to rotate 30 steps forward (relatively) and 30 steps in reverse continuously, like a windshield wiper on a car. Both programs drive the stepper as shown in Figure 5–14 using port 1.

The programs shown in Figures 5–17 and 5–18 use a table of drive codes and a pointer to the table in order to keep track of the current step (position in the table). Another counter is used to count the 30 steps in each direction, and a flag is used to control the direction.

```
1        ; Stepper Motor Driver.
2        dflag   equ     20h         ;direction flag
3                org     2000h
4        start:  ljmp    init
5
6        delay:  mov     tmod,#21h ;set timer mode
7                mov     th0,#0b8h ;approx 20 millisecs
8                mov     tl0,#00h
9                clr     tf0         ;clear rollover flag
10               setb    tr0         ;turn on timer 0
11       tloop:  jnb     tf0,tloop ;wait for rollover
12               clr     tr0         ;turn timer off
13               ret
14
15       steptab:db      0ah,08h,09h,01h,05h,04h,06h,02h
16
17       init:   clr     dflag       ;set initial direction
18               mov     r1,#0       ;starting step number
19               mov     dptr,#steptab
20       loop:   mov     r0,#30      ;number of steps
21       lupe:   mov     a,r1        ;get step number
22               movc    a,@a+dptr ;get drive code
23               mov     p1,a        ;output drive
24               acall   delay       ;wait 8 msecs.
25               jnb     dflag,ccw ;jump if clear
26               inc     r1          ;count up by 1
27               sjmp    l1          ;jump around decrement
28       ccw:    dec     r1          ;count down by one
29       l1:     anl     01,#07h     ;mask for 7 max count
30               djnz    r0,lupe     ;next step
31               cpl     dflag       ;change direction
32               sjmp    loop        ;restart
33               end
```

FIGURE 5–17 Assembly-language stepper motor driver.

```
1    #include <c:\c51\reg52.h>
2
3    void time()
4      {
5      TH0 = 0x01; /* 20 millisecond delay */
6      TL0 = 0x00;
7      TF0 = 0;      /* clear rollover flag */
8      TR0 = 1;      /* turn timer on */
9      while (TF0 == 0); /* wait for roll over */
10     TR0 = 0;      /* timer off */
11     }
12
13   unsigned char steptab[] =
          {0xa,0x8,0x9,0x1,0x5,0x4,0x6,0x2};
14
15   main()
16     {
17     unsigned char ptr = 0; /*step counter*/
18     unsigned char cntr; /*loop counter*/
19     bit DFLAG; /*direction flag*/
20     TMOD = 0x21;   /* gate=0, mode 1*/
21     DFLAG = 0; /*set initial direction*/
22     while (1)
23       {
24       for (cntr=0;cntr<30;cntr++)
25         {
26         P1 = steptab[ptr & 0x7]; /*output step code*/
27         time(); /*wait 20 msecs*/
28         if (DFLAG==0) ptr++; /*increment step counter*/
29         else ptr--; /*decrement step counter*/
30         }
31       DFLAG = !(DFLAG); /*change direction*/
32       }
33     }
```

FIGURE 5–18 C-language stepper motor driver.

The direct-drive method of stepper motor control requires that the microcontroller be largely dedicated to driving the stepper motor or motors, because of the timing requirements to run one or more stepper motors. While there are software techniques to improve the microcontroller's ability to handle the job, there is also a hardware solution. Intelligent stepper motor drivers exist that relieve the microcontroller of a part of the task. Figure 5–19 shows one such driver, made by Sprague.

FIGURE 5–19 Stepper motor driver interface.

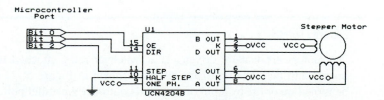

```
1          ;Stepper Motor Driver.
2          dflag    equ     91h      ;direction bit
3          step     equ     90H      ;step bit
4                   org     2000h
5          start:   ljmp    init
6
7          delay:   mov     tmod,#21h ;set timer mode
8                   mov     th0,#0b8h ;approx 20 millisecs
9                   mov     tl0,#00h
10                  clr     tf0      ;clear rollover flag
11                  setb    tr0      ;turn on timer 0
12         tloop:   jnb     tf0,tloop ;wait for rollover
13                  clr     tr0      ;turn timer off
14                  ret
15
16         init:    clr     dflag    ;set initial direction
17         loop:    mov     r0,#30   ;number of steps
18         lupe:    setb    step     ;make pulse
19                  clr     step
20                  acall   delay    ;wait for step to occur
21                  djnz    r0,lupe  ;next step
22                  cpl     dflag    ;change direction
23                  sjmp    loop     ;restart
24                  end
```

FIGURE 5–20   Modified assembly-language stepper motor driver.

The driver shown in Figure 5–19 relieves the microcontroller of the need to output the drive codes and to track the current step number within a table of output codes. It also contains the driver transistors and requires only two inputs to function. The two inputs are *step* and *direction*. A high or low on the direction input will control the rotational direction, and a pulse on the step input will cause one step to occur. The driver shown also has an Output Enable (OE) to allow shutting off the motor current between steps if no holding torque is required. Holding torque (current flowing) may be required if the motor is to hold its position against some mechanical force. It is not required if no such force exists. It is not used in the programs shown and is assumed to be tied to logic high.

The programs of Figures 5–17 and 5–18 are shown in Figures 5–20 and 5–21, respectively, as modified to work with the intelligent driver chip. These programs output the step signal on port 1, bit 0, and the direction signal on port 1, bit 1.

These two programs show clearly the reduction in programming that is allowed by use of the intelligent driver circuit. Note that the time delay between steps must still be provided by the software. This small programming cost allows the driver to be used with a variety of stepper motors.

5–6   DC MOTORS

DC motors are usually driven via a switch or relay attached to a parallel port on the microcontroller. The transistor interface shown in Figure 5–22 will allow the motor to be turned on or off by a pin of the microcontroller's parallel port. Outputting a logic high

```
1   #include <c:\c51\reg52.h>
2   sbit STEP=0x90;  /* P1.0 bit*/
3   sbit DIRECTION=0x91; /*P1.1 bit*/
4
5   void time()
6     {
7     TH0 = 0xb8; /* 20 millisecond delay */
8     TL0 = 0x00;
9     TF0 = 0;      /* clear rollover flag */
10    TR0 = 1;      /* turn timer on */
11    while (TF0 == 0); /* wait for roll over */
12    TR0 = 0;      /* timer off */
13    }
14
15  main()
16    {
17    unsigned char cntr; /*loop counter*/
18    TMOD = 0x21;  /* gate=0, mode 1*/
19    DIRECTION = 0; /*set initial direction*/
20    while (1)
21      {
22      for (cntr=0;cntr<30;cntr++)
23        {
24        STEP = 1; /*make step pulse*/
25        STEP = 0;
26        time(); /*wait 20 msecs*/
27        }
28      DIRECTION = !(DIRECTION); /*change direction*/
29      }
30    }
```

FIGURE 5–21   Modified C-language stepper motor driver.

FIGURE 5–22   DC motor
interface.

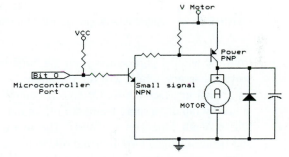

FIGURE 5–23   PWM speed
control.

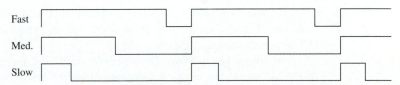

```
 1          ; PWM Motor Driver.
 2          Motor    equ     90H         ;Motor control bit
 3          Speed    equ     90H         ;speed control port
 4
 5                   org     2000h
 6          init:    sjmp    start       ;jump to program
 7
 8          msec:    mov     tmod,#21h ;set timer mode
 9                   mov     th0,#0ffh ;approx 100 microsecs
10                   mov     tl0,#0a4h
11                   clr     tf0         ;clear rollover flag
12                   setb    tr0         ;turn on timer 0
13          tloop:   jnb     tf0,tloop ;wait for rollover
14                   clr     tr0         ;turn timer off
15                   ret
16
17          start:   mov     a,P1        ;read speed control
18                   anl     a,#0e0h     ;mask excess bits
19          chkfst:  cjne    a,#80h,chkmed ;fast ?
20                   mov     r0,#90      ;load for fast
21                   mov     r1,#10
22                   sjmp    run         ;go run motor
23          chkmed:  cjne    a,#40h,chkslo ;slow?
24                   mov     r0,#50      ;load for medium
25                   mov     r1,#50
26                   sjmp    run         ;go run motor
27          chkslo:  cjne    a,#20h,start ;slow?
28                   mov     r0,#10      ;load for slow
29                   mov     r1,#90
30          run:     setb    motor       ;motor on
31          loop1:   acall   msec        ;wait 1 mse
32                   djnz    r0,loop1    ;wait out on time
33                   clr     motor       ;motor off
34          loop2:   acall   msec        ;wait 1 msec
35                   djnz    r1,loop2    ;wait out off time
36                   sjmp    start
37                   end
```

FIGURE 5–24 Assembly-language PWM control.

from the parallel port will turn on the NPN transistor. This will then turn on the PNP power transistor, which will run the motor.

This interface allows for on–off control. It is possible to control the speed of the motor by rapidly turning the motor off and on and controlling the proportion of on-time (Pulse-Width Modulation, PWM). The motor cannot start and stop as quickly as the microcontroller can turn it on and off, so the motor assumes a speed approximately equal to the average voltage applied to it. Figure 5–23 shows three possible cases to illustrate this point.

Figures 5–24 and 5–25 show programs that read the logic level inputs at P1, bits 5, 6, and 7, and then provide pulse-width speed control at P1, bit 0, according to the I/O bit set as shown in Figure 5–26.

Although the programs shown provide only three discrete speeds, the general concept of PWM control can be used with many discrete levels of control. The concept is also applicable to dimming lamps, LEDs, and other devices where the average current or

```
1   #include <c:\c51\reg52.h>
2   #define SPEED P1
3   sbit MOTOR=0x90;   /* P1.0 bit*/
4
5   void time()
6     {
7     TH0 = 0xff;  /* 100 microsecond delay */
8     TL0 = 0xa4;
9     TF0 = 0;     /* clear rollover flag */
10    TR0 = 1;     /* turn timer on */
11    while (TF0 == 0); /* wait for roll over */
12    TR0 = 0;     /* timer off */
13    }
14
15  main()
16    {
17    unsigned char t1,x; /*ontime,loop counter*/
18    while (1)
19      {
20      if ((SPEED & 0xe0)==0x80)t1=90;
21      if ((SPEED & 0xe0)==0x40)t1=50;
22      if ((SPEED & 0xe0)==0x20)t1=10;
23      if (t1>0)
24        {
25        MOTOR=1; /*motor on*/
26        for (x=0;x<t1;x++) time();
27        MOTOR=0; /*motor off*/
28        for (x=t1;x<100;x++) time();
29        t1=0; /*clear time counter*/
30        }
31      }
32    }
```

FIGURE 5–25   C-language PWM control.

FIGURE 5–26   Speed control input/outputs.

Bit Set	Speed
7	Fast (90% duty cycle)
6	Medium (50% duty cycle)
5	Slow (10% duty cycle)

voltage applied controls speed, brightness, and so on. A more complete PWM system is discussed in Chapter 6.

5–7   SUMMARY

The 8051 may be used with a variety of external peripherals. Analog-to-digital and digital-to-analog converters may be used to interface the 8051 to analog signals and devices. Liquid-crystal displays are used to display alphanumeric data, and hex keypads are often used as input I/O devices with the 8051 embedded controllers. Higher-visibility displays may be constructed using seven-segment LED displays.

For motion control, stepper motors interface directly to the 8051 or may be interfaced via intelligent driver circuits. Motive power may be provided by pulse-width driving DC motors. These devices present the range of the more common interfaces; many additional peripherals may be interfaced to the 8051 through similar means.

5-8   EXERCISES

1. Calculate the voltage resolution of a 10-bit ADC with a full-scale measurement range of 5 V.
2. Calculate the voltage resolution of an 8-bit ADC with a full-scale measurement range of 10 V.
3. Calculate the output voltage of a 12-bit DAC (full-scale output of 12 V) for each of the following digital inputs:

$$0x1ce$$

$$0x734$$

$$0x34d$$

4. Using the circuit of Figure 5–6, determine the key pressed for the following conditions:

Col Input				Row Output				Key Pressed
C1	C2	C3	C4	R1	R2	R3	R4	
1	0	1	1	1	1	0	1	_____
0	1	1	1	1	0	1	1	_____
1	1	1	0	0	1	1	1	_____

5. Define the difference between a stepper motor and a DC motor. Which of the two motors would be appropriate to provide motive power for the drive motors of a computer-controlled car? Which would be best to provide the steering? Why?
6. Extend Figure 5–11 to include the letters P, U, r, d, and E.
7. Calculate the peak current for a scanned seven-segment display consisting of three digits. Assume that the digits can withstand 18 mA of average current flow.
8. Determine a suitable interface circuit to attach a synthesized music circuit to the 8051 system of Figure 5–1. Use an on-bus interface. The synthesizer requires 8 bits of data to determine its function, and it needs a negative-going pulse to latch data into the device. No other interface signals are required.

CHAPTER 6

Advanced Topics

OVERVIEW

This chapter covers a variety of advanced topics that are important to effective development of 8051-based projects. The topics covered include interrupts, multiprocessor systems, and power control.

6–1 INTERRUPTS

Interrupts are external or internal hardware events that cause the microprocessor to branch away from the normal program flow to answer an immediate need. Interrupts are analogous to subroutine calls in that the normal flow of the program is interrupted while the interrupt completes its task, after which the flow of the program is resumed. Interrupts are useful for events that require immediate attention (a keyboard or a safety feature) or for events that occur sporadically, making it inefficient for the microcontroller to poll for the event.

As an example of a time-critical case, a robot controlled by an 8031 controller might need to change its direction immediately when it bumps into something. An interrupt could be used with the bumpers so that the robot's controller could be busy controlling the robot motion until the interrupt event (bumping into something) occurs, then the interrupt service routine (a piece of program code very similar to a subroutine) would be responsible to reverse the robot's direction of travel before returning control to the main program.

An interrupt may be caused by any of several events, such as an external logic signal going low, an internal timer rolling over to 0x0000, or the receipt of a serial character on the serial port. Each interrupt may be enabled or disabled by the programmer to suit the particular needs of the project.

When an interrupt occurs, the microcontroller branches to an address assigned to that interrupt and executes the special program code to *service* the interrupt. This piece of code (the interrupt service routine) is written by the programmer and is very much like a subroutine in form. In fact, the interrupt functions almost exactly like a subroutine except that the interrupt is "called" by a hardware event. The sequence is:

1. The interrupt event occurs.
2. The microcontroller completes the current instruction cycle.
3. The contents of the PC (the next instruction to be executed after the interrupt service routine) are stored on the stack.
4. The microcontroller branches to an assigned address, which must hold either the program code written to service the interrupt or a jump instruction that branches to the service routine code.
5. Upon completion of the interrupt service routine, the microcontroller returns to the program that was being executed when the interrupt occurred by retrieving the address stored on the stack and placing it into the PC. The program continues executing from the point in the program at which it branched.

There are five possible sources of interrupts in the 8051 family of microcontrollers, two external and three internal. External interrupts may be either level or edge triggered by logic signals applied to the INTerrupt 0 (INT0) or INTerrupt 1 (INT1) pins. Internal events that can cause an interrupt are the rollover (transition from 0xffff to 0x0000) of either counter or the completion of a complete transmission or reception of a serial word.

Each possible interrupt source has an associated vector address to which the processor branches when that particular interrupt occurs. Table 6–1 shows the interrupts, sources, causes, and associated vector addresses.

The vector addresses are spaced at intervals of 8 bytes. Since it is unlikely that the entire interrupt service routine can be placed into the 8 bytes available at the vector address, the usual practice is to provide a jump at the vector address, which then causes a branch to the actual service routine.

Interrupts must be enabled in order to function. The Interrupt Enable (IE) special function register is used to control the interrupts. Each interrupt has one bit associated with it that must be set (unmasked) for the interrupt to be used. One additional bit, the Enable All (EA) bit, must also be set high for any interrupts to operate. The EA bit may

TABLE 6–1   Interrupt causes and vector addresses

Interrupt	Source	Cause	Vector Address
External interrupt 0	INT0 pin	Low level or falling edge (selectable)	0x0003
Timer 0	TF0	Rollover from 0xffff to 0x0000	0x000B
External interrupt 1	INT1 pin	Low level or falling edge (selectable)	0x0013
Timer 1	TF1	Rollover from 0xffff to 0x0000	0x001B
Serial port	RI or TI	Completion of transmission or reception of a word	0x0023

IE Interrupt Enable Register

(msb)   (lsb)

EA			ES	ET1	EX1	ET0	EX0

EA   Enable All
ES   Enable Serial Interrupt
ET1   Enable Timer 1 Interrupt
EX1   Enable External Interrupt 1
ET0   Enable Timer 0 Interrupt
EX0   Enable External Interrupt 0

IP Interrupt Priority Register

(msb)   (lsb)

			PS	PT1	PX1	PT0	PX0

PS   Priority of the Serial Interrupt
PT1   Priority of the Timer 1 Interrupt
PX1   Priority of External Interrupt 1
PT0   Priority of the Timer 0 Interrupt
PX0   Priority of External Interrupt 0

FIGURE 6–1   Interrupt registers.

be used to enable or disable those interrupts that are enabled by having their control bits set high.

The 8051 interrupts may also be prioritized to determine the order in which interrupts will be serviced. The 8051 family microcontrollers allows for two priority levels associated with each interrupt. Each interrupt may be set as either a low-priority interrupt (the default state) or a high-priority interrupt. A high-priority interrupt may interrupt a low-priority interrupt, but interrupts of the same priority may not interrupt each other, nor may low-priority interrupts interrupt high-priority interrupts. Setting an interrupt to high priority requires setting its associated bit in the Interrupt Priority (IP) special function register.

The bit definitions for IP and IE are identical except for the EA bit. See Figure 6–1 for bit definitions and Table 6–2 for brief examples.

Programming to use interrupts in assembly code requires special attention. Since it is not possible to know which part of a program may be executing when an interrupt occurs, it is very important that the interrupt service routines *must not* change the contents of any registers. Consequently, most interrupt service routines begin with a series of *push* instructions to save all the registers that might be altered by the service routine; and they end with a corresponding series of *pop* instructions to restore the registers the service routine has modified. The example programs do not modify any registers as a part of the service routine, so it is not necessary to save the contents of any registers in these cases. It is also important to note that service routines in assembly code must end with an RETI instruction to clear the interrupt priority system upon completion. High-level languages

TABLE 6–2   Interrupt enabling examples

IE	IP	Results
00001001	00000000	No interrupts enabled (EA = 0)
10001001	00000000	External 0 and timer 1 interrupts enabled—no priority
10001001	00001000	Same as above except timer 1 has high priority

such as C take care of these details for the programmer. Programming examples of both external and internal interrupts are given in the sections that follow.

External Interrupts

External interrupts are associated with microcontroller pins INT0 and INT1. These interrupts may be caused by either a low level or a falling edge at the pin, depending on the control bits in the TCON. Bit 0 of the TCON is the control bit (IT0) for external interrupt 0. If IT0 is set, the interrupt will occur only on a falling edge at the INT0 pin. If IT0 is cleared, any low-level signal on INT0 will cause the interrupt to occur. Bit 2 of the TCON is the control bit (IT1) for external interrupt 1 and works identically.

The advantage to using an edge-triggered interrupt is that the interrupt will be triggered only once each time the interrupt goes low. Without edge triggering, interrupt signals lasting longer than the interrupt service routine would cause multiple interrupts to occur. Interrupt software is illustrated in Figure 6–2 and 6–3, which show identical programs written in assembly and C language. The programs demonstrate the use of

```
1       ;External Interrupts
2               org     0000h
3       start:  ljmp    init    ;jump around interrupts
4
5               org     0003h   ;interrupt 0
6               ljmp    srvice0 ;jump to irupt 0 service
7               org     0013h   ;interrupt 1
8       srvice1:setb    p1.0    ;set p1 bit 0
9               reti            ;return from interrupt
10      srvice0:clr     p1.0    ;clear p1 bit 0
11              reti            ;return from interrupt
12
13      delay:  mov     b,#10   ;1/2 second
14      del2:   mov     th0,#4ch;50 millisecs delay time
15              mov     tl0,#00h
16              clr     tf0     ;clear rollover flag
17              setb    tr0     ;turn on timer 0
18      tloop:  jnb     tf0,tloop;wait for rollover
19              clr     tr0     ;turn timer off
20              djnz    b,del2  ;loop until delay done
21              ret
22
23      init:   setb    IT0     ;make EX0 edge triggerred
24              clr     IT1     ;make EX1 level triggerred
25              mov     IE,#85h ;set EA, EX1, and EX2
26              mov     IP,#01h ;give EX0 priority
27      lupe:   setb    p1.7    ;set blinker bit
28              acall   delay   ;wait 1/2 sec
29              clr     p1.7    ;clear blinker bit
30              acall   delay   ;wait 1/2 second
31              sjmp    lupe    ;repaet forever
32
33              end
```

FIGURE 6–2   External interrupts in assembly language.

```
1     #include <c:\c51\reg52.h>
2     sbit P1_0=0x90;
3     sbit P1_1=0x91;
4     sbit BLINK=0x97;
5
6     void ext0() interrupt 0 using 2
7      {
8      P1_0 = 0;   /*clear p1.0*/
9      }
10    void ext1() interrupt 2 using 2
11     {
12     P1_0 = 1;   /*set p1.0*/
13     }
14
15    void time()
16      {
17      unsigned char x; /*time delay counter*/
18      for (x=0;x<20;x++)
19        {
20        TH0 = 0x4c; /* 50 millisecond delay */
21        TL0 = 0x00;
22        TF0 = 0;     /* clear rollover flag */
23        TR0 = 1;     /* turn timer on */
24        while (TF0 == 0); /* wait for roll over */
25        TR0 = 0;     /* timer off */
26        }
27      }
28
29    main()
30      {
31      IT0=0x1; /*external 0 edge triggerred*/
32      IT1=0x0; /*external 1 edge triggerred*/
33      IE=0x85; /*enable EX0 and EX1*/
34      IP=0x01; /*set EX0 to high priority*/
35      while (1)
36        {
37        BLINK = 1; /*set blinker on*/
38        time(); /*wait 1/2 second*/
39        BLINK = 0; /*set blinker off*/
40        time(); /*wait 1/2 second*/
41        }
42      }
```

FIGURE 6-3 External interrupts in C language.

external interrupts. Each program has as its main task to toggle the most significant bit of port 1 at a $\frac{1}{2}$-s rate. The programs enable external interrupts 0 and 1. External interrupt 0 is initialized as an edge-triggered, high-priority interrupt. External interrupt 1 is initialized as a level-triggered, low-priority interrupt.

The programs operate as follows. The main program loop continuously complements bit 7 of port 1 at a $\frac{1}{2}$-s rate. When a low-going edge is detected on INT0, the program branches to the service routine and clears the least significant bit of port 1. When a low level is detected on INT1, the least significant bit of port 1 is set high. If both interrupts occur at exactly the same instant, INT0 has higher priority and the least significant bit of

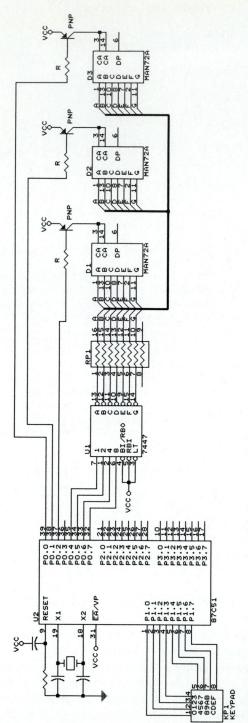

FIGURE 6–4 Keypad and display system example.

port 1 is cleared. However, since INT0 is set for edge triggering, its interrupt occurs only once and then (assuming that the low level is still applied to INT1) the INT1 interrupt occurs and the bit is immediately set. If INT1 occurs while INT0 is working, its low priority will cause it to be ignored unless the INT1 signal lasts past the end of the SRVICE0 routine. On the other hand, if INT0 occurs while INT1 is working, the higher-priority interrupt will prevail and the least significant bit of port 1 will be cleared.

Timer Interrupts

There are two timer interrupts in the 8051 family of microcontrollers, which occur when either timer rolls over from all 1s to all 0s. The timer interrupts are caused by the operation of the TFx bit for either counter. When either counter rolls over to 0x0000, its timer flag bit is set and an interrupt is generated if the interrupt for that particular counter is enabled. When the interrupt occurs, the program branches to an appropriate service routine at the address specified in Table 6–1.

The timer interrupts are especially useful for creating a time base for operations that need to be accomplished regularly. Examples are scanning a hex keypad, scanning a seven-segment display, or updating a real-time clock. In the application shown in Figure 6–4, a timer is set to time out or rollover at a regular rate (10 ms in this example). Whenever the rollover occurs, time-critical operations may be carried out without disturbing the main program.

Figures 6–5 and 6–6 show examples of time-based programs in which the timer interrupts are used to scan seven-segment displays and a keypad. The two programs work identically. They continuously scan a three-digit seven-segment display, scan a hex keypad, and keep track of real time in seconds. The seconds that have elapsed are shown on two digits of the scanned seven-segment display, and the last key pressed on the keypad is displayed on the third digit.

The main program (starting at line 73 of the assembly-language program and line 64 of the C program) initializes timer 0 to be a 16-bit timer and then loads the counters for a 10-ms time-out. The timer 0 run bit (TR0) is then set to start the timer running. The IE register is loaded with 0x82 to enable the timer 0 interrupt, and the program variables are initialized. Then the main program enters an infinite do-nothing loop. In a more realistic program, code would replace the do-nothing loop so that the microcontroller could be busy doing constructive work whenever it was not servicing the interrupt.

The interrupt service routine is the key to the operation of this program. The service routine starts at line 8 of the assembly-language routine and line 43 of the C program. The service routine first must reload the timer for the next 10-ms time-out. It then updates a counter that is counting the number of 10-ms ''ticks.'' When this count reaches 100, one second has passed (100×10 ms $= 1$ s) and the seconds counter variable is incremented. This counter actually keeps track of the 1s digit of the elapsed seconds. It is then checked to see if it is equal to 10 and, if so, it is cleared and the 10s-of-seconds counter is updated. This counter is also checked to see if it is equal to 10 and, if so, it is cleared. The two counters keeping track of the seconds and 10s of seconds are stored at locations known to the display routine so that the digits may be displayed.

Next the service routine scans the hex keypad; if a key is pressed, the value of the key is placed in a memory location known to the display routine for display. The hex keypad scanner routines are virtually the same as presented in Chapter 5, except that the

```
 1 ;Keypad scanning program.
 3            org     2000h
 4 start:     ljmp    init     ;jump to main program
 5            org     000bh    ;start of interrupt service code
 8 tick:      mov     th0,#0dch;reload for 10ms
 9            mov     tl0,#00h
10 clock:     inc     r2       ;incr 10's ms counter
11            cjne    r2,#100,scan;jump if not 1 sec
12            mov     r2,#00h  ;clear r2
13            mov     a#10     ;comparison number
14            inc     20h      ;bump seconds count
16            cjne    a,20h,scan;jump if not 10
17            mov     20h,#0   ;clear secs count
18            inc     21h      ;bump tens of secs count
20            cjne    a,21h,scan;jump if not 10
21            mov     21h,#0   ;clear tens of secs count
22 scan:      mov     a,#0feh  ;beginning pattern
23 lup:       mov     r5,a     ;save output pattern
24            mov     P1,a     ;output pattern
25            mov     a,P1     ;read port
26            mov     r1,a     ;save keyread
27            orl     a,#0fh   ;set drive bits high
28            cjne    a,#0ffh,cnvrt ;jump if key pressed
29            mov     a,r5     ;recover drive
30            rl      a        ;rotate drive bit left
31            cjne    a,#0efh,lup ;jump to scan next col
32            sjmp    disply   ;no keys pressed-jump to display
33 cnvrt:     mov     a,r1     ;recover keyread
34            mov     r3,#0    ;clear table counter
35 clup:      jnb     acc.0,cnvrt2;done with major count
36            rr      a        ;rotate value
37            mov     r6,a     ;save rotated value
38            mov     a,r3     ;incr counter
39            add     a,#4     ;add 4 per column
40            mov     r3,a     ;save count
41            mov     a,r6     ;recover rotating value
42            sjmp    clup
43 cnvrt2:    mov     a,r1     ;recover keyread
44            swap    a        ;exchange nybbles to get rows
45 clup2:     jnb     acc.0,xlat;jump to translate reading
46            rr      a        ;rotate to find zero
47            inc     r3       ;bump counter
48            sjmp    clup2    ;jump to check next bit
49 xlat:      mov     a,r3     ;get count
50            mov     dptr,#keytab ;point to translate table
51            movc    a,@a+dptr;get translated character
52            mov     22h,a    ;put char to display in ml22
53 disply:    mov     a,r0     ;get display counter
57            add     a,#20h   ;add offset to display digits
58            mov     r1,a     ;put in digit pointer
59            mov     a,@r1    ;get digit to display
60            swap    a        ;mov to upper nybble
61            mov     r4,a     ;save it
62            mov     a,r0     ;get counter again
```

FIGURE 6–5 Assembly-language time-base program.

```
63              mov     dptr,#drvtab;point to drive table
64              movc    a,@a+dptr;get drive code
65              orl     a,r4       ;combine drive and digit
66              mov     P0,a       ;output it to display
67              inc     r0         ;bump digit counter
68              mov     a,#03      ;comparison value
69              cjne    a,00,noclr;jump if r0 not = 3
70              mov     r0,#0      ;clear digit counter
71 noclr:       reti               ;return from interrupt
72
73 init:        mov     tmod,#21h;enable T0 as a 16 bit counter
74              mov     th0,#0dch;counts for 10 ms.
75              mov     tl0,#00h
76              setb    tr0        ;start timer 0
77              mov     ie,#82h ;enable timer 0 interrupt
78              mov     r0,#0      ;clear digit counter
79              clr     a          ;clear acc
80              mov     20h,a      ;clear seconds counter
81              mov     21h,a      ;clear tens of seconds
82              mov     22h,a      ;clear button press digit
83 wate:        sjmp    wate       ;do nothing
84
85 keytab: db          0,4,8,0ch,1,5,9,0dh
86         db          2,6,0ah,0eh,3,7,0bh,0fh
87 drvtab: db          0eh,0dh,0bh
88
89              end
```

FIGURE 6–5 *continued*

assembly-language routine is modified so that it does not wait for a keypress, returning 0xff if no key is pressed.

The data are displayed on the seven-segment display by first getting the value of the next digit to be displayed, then shifting it 4 bits to the left, and finally combining it with the drive information for the digit to be illuminated. The new display information is then output to the display. In the assembly-language program the display digits are stored in three successive memory locations and the drive information is contained in a table. In this way a single register (R0) can be used as a pointer to both the digit and the drive. In the C program an array is used for both, so that a single counter (dispcounter) may also be used to point to each array.

It may appear that considerable time is being spent in the interrupt service routine. In fact, less than 60 μs are used by the assembly-language service routine, and less than twice that by the C-language service routine. Since the routine is executed only once every 10 ms, the worst case (the C-program service routine) is that the service routine uses only 1.2% of the available time. Clearly, the microcontroller can accomplish many things besides the service routine.

Serial Interrupts

The serial interrupt in the 8031 family occurs for two separate events, when a serial word is received and when a serial word has been fully transmitted. Using the interrupts associated with the serial port is important, since the port can only transmit or receive a

```
1        #define KEYPAD P1
2        #include <c:\c51\reg52.h>
3        #include <c:\c51\absacc.h>
4        unsigned char dispcounter;  /*disp. posit. counter*/
5        unsigned char mscounter; /*tens of ms counter*/
6        unsigned char seconds; /*secs counter*/
7        unsigned char tseconds; /*tens secs counter*/
8        unsigned char dispdigits[3]; /*display array*/
9        code unsigned char drivetab[] = {0x0e, 0x0d, 0x0b};
                                /* digit drive table*/
10
11       unsigned char scan()
12          {
13          unsigned char scandrive = 0xfe; /*scanner drive*/
14          unsigned char count = 0;/*counter for conversion*/
15          unsigned char key, majorkey, minorkey;
16          code unsigned char keytab[] =
             {0,4,8,0xc,1,5,9,0xd,2,6,0xa,0xe,3,7,0xb,0xf};
17          key = 0xf0; /*preset key*/
18          while ((scandrive != 0xef)&&((key & 0XF0)==0XF0))
19             {
20             KEYPAD = scandrive; /*output drive*/
21             key = KEYPAD; /*read keypad*/
22             scandrive=(scandrive*2)+1; /*shift drive left*/
23             }
24          if (key == 0xf7) return 0xff; /*key not pressed*/
25          else
26             {
27             majorkey = key; /*get key and drive code*/
28             while ((majorkey & 0x01) != 0)
29                {
30                count = count + 4; /*increment major count*/
31                majorkey=(majorkey>>1);/*shift right 1 bit*/
32                }
33             minorkey=(key >> 4);/*get minor key and drive*/
34             while ((minorkey & 0x01) != 0)
35                {
36                count++; /*increment minor count*/
37                minorkey = (minorkey >> 1); /*shift right*/
38                }
39             return keytab[count]; /*translate key press*/
40             }
41          }
42
43       void ct0() interrupt 1 using 2
44          {
45          unsigned char tempchar; /*temporary variable*/
46          TH0 = 0xdc;  /*reload for 10ms.*/
47          TL0 = 0x00;
48          if ((++mscounter) == 100)
                /*increment and check tens millisecs counter*/
49             {
50             mscounter=0; /*clear tens of millisecs counter*/
51             if ((++seconds) == 10)
```

FIGURE 6–6 C-language time base-program.

```
                       /*increment and check seconds counter*/
52                     {
53                     seconds=0; /*clear seconds counter*/
54                     if ((++tseconds) == 10) tseconds = 0;
                           /*clear tens secs counter*/
55                     }
56                 }
57             dispdigits[0]=seconds; /*reload display digits*/
58             dispdigits[1]=tseconds; /*likewise*/
59             if (scan() != 0xff) dispdigits[2] = scan();
                   /*load new keystroke*/
60             P0 = ((dispdigits[dispcounter] * 16) +
                   drivetab[dispcounter]); /*output*/
61             if ((++dispcounter) == 0x03) dispcounter = 0;
                   /*increment & restart display counter*/
62         }

63
64     main()
65         {
66         unsigned char x;
67         TMOD = 0x21; /*initialize Timer 0*/
68         TH0 = 0xdc; /*preload counters for 10 ms*/
69         TL0 = 0x00;
70         TR0 = 1; /*turn on timer 0*/
71         IE = 0x82; /*enable timer 0 interrupt*/
72         dispcounter = 0; /*clear display counter*/
73         for ( x=0; x<3; x++) dispdigits[x]=0;
74         seconds = 0; /*clear time counters*/
75         tseconds = 0;
76         mscounter = 0;
77         while (1); /*do nothing forever*/
78         }
```

FIGURE 6–6   *continued*

word approximately every 1 ms (at 9600 baud), and so it would be inefficient for the microcontroller to wait for each of these events. The interrupt-on-receive allows the microcontroller to respond promptly to serial information, and the interrupt-on-transmit permits the microcontroller to transmit a series of serial words without waiting around for the serial port between transmissions.

Since the serial interrupt occurs for two different events, the service routine must sort out the cause of the interrupt before acting. Figures 6–7 and 6–8 show programs that demonstrate the serial interrupt. Each initializes the serial port and then enables the serial interrupt.

When the interrupt occurs, the service routine first checks to see if the interrupt was caused by the transmitter or the receiver. If the interrupt resulted from the transmitter, the TI bit is cleared and the service routine ends. If the interrupt resulted from the receipt of a serial character, the character is read and sent to the transmitter to echo it.

In a more extensive system, the serial interrupt service routine might use the occurrence of the transmit-complete interrupt to transmit the next in a series of characters, or the receive-complete interrupt to signal the main loop to stop its activities to receive new commands or data.

```
 1            org     0000h
 2 start:     ljmp    init
 3            org     0023h       ;serial interrupt vector
 4 serserv:jb         ti,xmit     ;jump if caused by xmit
 5 rcv:       clr     ri          ;clear receive flag
 6            mov     a,sbuf      ;get character
 7            mov     sbuf,a      ;echo it serially
 8            reti
 9 xmit:      clr     ti          ;clear xmit flag
10            reti
11
12 init:      mov     scon,#50h ;8 bin UART, RCV enabled
13            mov     tmod,#20h ;set timer 1 mode 1
14            mov     tcon,#0   ;nothing running
15            mov     th1,#0fdh ;reload value
16            setb    tr1         ;start timer 1
17            mov     ie,#90h     ;enable serial interrupt
18 wate:      sjmp    wate        ;do-nothing loop
19            end
```

FIGURE 6–7   Assembly-language serial interrupt program.

```
 1       #include <c:\c51\reg52.h>
 2
 3       void ser() interrupt 4 using 1
 4          {
 5          if (TI != 1)
 6             {
 7             RI = 0; /*clear receive flag*/
 8             SBUF = SBUF; /*echo the received character*/
 9             }
10          else TI = 0; /*clear transmit flag*/
11          }
12
13       main()
14          {
15          SCON = 0x50; /*8-bit UART, RCV enabled*/
16          TMOD = 0x20; /*timer 1 mode 1*/
17          TCON = 0x00; /*nothing running*/
18          TR1 = 1; /*timer on*/
19          IE = 0x90; /*enable serial interrupt*/
20          while (1); /*do-nothing loop*/
21          }
```

FIGURE 6–8   C-language serial interrupt program.

6–2   MULTIPROCESSOR SYSTEMS

The 8051 family of microcontrollers incorporates a special feature to allow the use of multiple processors working together. This feature allows the use of a single-wire serial communication system that differentiates between address information and data traveling on the serial bus. The communication system requires a ''master'' and ''slave'' arrangement on the serial bus. The master is responsible for establishing communication with any desired slave processor. After communication is established, slaves that are not participating in the communication simply ignore the serial data and carry on with their tasks.

The master establishes communication by sending out the address of the slave with which communication is desired. The address byte is marked by the ninth bit being set high while data bytes have this bit set low. The slaves use the multiprocessor communication feature that prevents their serial port from generating an interrupt from any received word whose ninth bit is set low. In this way data bytes do not cause an interrupt in the slaves not being addressed, leaving them free to continue their tasks. All the slaves must process the interrupt from an address byte, but only the slave whose address matches that sent by the master will disable the multiprocessor communication feature and allow its serial port to generate an interrupt for serial data words so that it can communicate with the master. The multiprocessor communication feature is controlled by the SM2 bit in the SCON register.

Both the master and the slaves must be using serial communication mode 2 or mode 3. The only difference between the modes is the method of setting their baud rate. Mode 2 is the fixed baud rate (the actual baud rate depends on the system crystal) option and

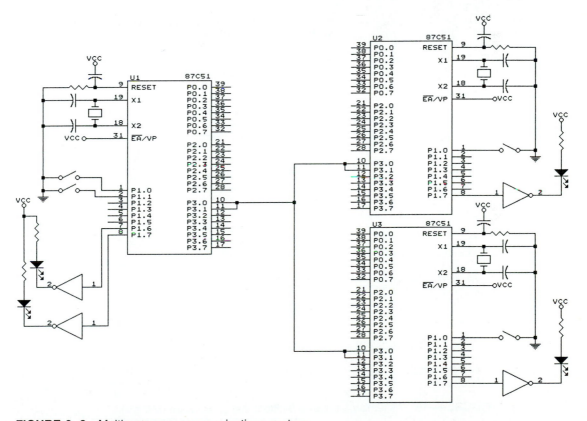

FIGURE 6-9 Multiprocessor communications system.

communicates using a 9-bit word plus start and stop bits. The ninth bit is controlled by the TB8 bit in the SCON in the master. When the master wishes to establish communication with a slave, it sets TB8 high and transmits the address. All of the slaves are interrupted and the slave whose address matches the one transmitted then sets its SM2 low. This disables its multiprocessor communication feature and allows every serial word on the bus to cause an interrupt in that slave only. The master sets its TB8 low so that further transmissions will not be treated as addresses and cause interrupts in the other slaves. At

```
 1           org       0000h
 2 start:    sjmp      init
 3
 4 xmitad:   setb      tb8        ;transmit addr
 5           sjmp      sendit     ;jump around data xmit
 6 xmitdat:  clr       tb8        ;set for data xmit
 7 sendit:   mov       sbuf,a     ;transmit word
 8 wateti:   jnb       ti,wateti  ;wait for transmit
 9           clr       ti         ;clear ti
10 wateri:   jnb       ri,wateri  ;wait for xmit to be r'cvd
11           clr       ri         ;clear from xmit
12           ret
13
14 init:     mov       scon,#98h  ;9 bit UART, RCV enabled, TB8=1
15 loop:     mov       a,#01h     ;load address
16           acall     xmitad     ;send address
17           mov       a,p1       ;get data
18           anl       a,#01h     ;mask unused bits
19           acall     xmitdat    ;send data
20
21 wateri1:  jnb       ri,wateri1 ;wait for return data
22           clr       ri         ;clear ri
23           mov       a,sbuf     ;get data character
24           jz        setlow     ;check output data
25           setb      p1.6       ;set if data high
26           sjmp      done       ;jump around clear
27 setlow:   clr       p1.6       ;clear data bit
28 done:     mov       a,#05h     ;load address
29           acall     xmitad     ;send address
30           mov       a,p1       ;get data
31           anl       a,#02h     ;mask unused bits
32           acall     xmitdat    ;send data
33
34 wateri5:  jnb       ri,wateri5 ;wait for return data
35           clr       ri         ;clear ri
36           mov       a,sbuf     ;get data character
37           jz        setlow5    ;check output data
38           setb      p1.7       ;set if data high
39           sjmp      done5      ;jump around clear
40 setlow5:  clr       p1.7       ;clear data bit
41 done5:    sjmp      loop       ;repeat operation
42           end
```

FIGURE 6–10　Assembly-language multiprocessor software (Master).

```
 1              org     0000h
 2  start:  mov     sp,#17h    ;set stack above user area
 3              mov     scon,#0b0h;8 bit UART, RCV enabled, sm2=1
 4              mov     ie,#90h    ;enable serial interrupt
 5  wate:   sjmp    wate       ;do-nothing loop
 6
 7              org     0023h      ;serial interrupt vector
 8  serserv:push    psw        ;save psw
 9              mov     psw,#010h  ;switch to bank 2
10              jb      ti,xmit    ;jump if caused by xmit
11  rcv:    clr     ri         ;clear receive flag
12              mov     a,sbuf     ;get character
13              cjne    a,#01h,notme;jump if wrong address
14              clr     sm2        ;eliminate multiproc mode
15  wateri: jnb     ri,wateri  ;wait for data word
16              clr     ri         ;clear ri from data
17              setb    sm2        ;reset multiproc mode
18              mov     a,sbuf     ;read data
19              jz      datalo     ;jump if low data
20              setb    p1.7       ;set data bit high
21              sjmp    doneset    ;jump the clear
22  datalo: clr     p1.7       ;data bit low
23  doneset:mov     a,p1       ;read switch
24              anl     a,#01h     ;mask other bits
25              mov     sbuf,a     ;transmit data
26              sjmp    notme      ;jump around clear
27  xmit:   clr     ti         ;clear xmit flag
28  notme:  pop     psw        ;see above
29              reti
30              end
```

FIGURE 6-10 *continued* (Slave 1)

the end of the master/slave communication sequence, the SM2 bit is again set high in the slave to prevent other data bytes from causing interrupts in the slave.

Figures 6-9 through 6-11 show a simple system and associated software that demonstrates the multiprocessor communications feature. Included are the master software and the software for each of two slaves. The programs use a master/slave communication configuration to pass data back and forth. Specifically, the master sends the data on its port 1, bit 0, to slave #1. Slave #1 displays this data on its port 1, bit 7, and returns the data from its port 1, bit 0, to the master. The master then displays this data on its port 1, bit 6. A similar loop exists for slave #2 (address 5), except that the data sent to #5 is from master port 1, bit 1, and the returned data is displayed on port 1, bit 7, of the master. In other words, toggle switches on the master control the LEDs on each slave, and the toggle switches connected to each slave control an LED on the master.

The master software is not interrupt driven, but rather polls the slaves, sending and receiving data in sequence. The slaves, however, are interrupt controlled. The master software sets up the serial port and then enters a loop in which the address of slave #1 (1) is transmitted followed by a data byte showing the state of its switch. Slave #1 lowers its SM2 upon receipt of its address (note that both slaves are interrupted to check the address byte) and then accepts the data byte and lights the LED according to the data

```
 1              org     0000h
 2  start:      mov     sp,#17h     ;set stack above user area
 3              mov     scon,#0b0h;8 bit UART, RCV enabled, sm2=1
 4              mov     ie,#90h     ;enable serial interrupt
 5  wate:       sjmp    wate        ;do-nothing loop
 6
 7              org     0023h       ;serial interrupt vector
 8  serserv:push        psw         ;save psw
 9              mov     psw,#010h   ;switch to bank 2
10              jb      ti,xmit     ;jump if caused by xmit
11  rcv:        clr     ri          ;clear receive flag
12              mov     a,sbuf      ;get character
13              cjne    a,#05h,notme;jump if wrong address
14              clr     sm2         ;eliminate multiproc mode
15  wateri:     jnb     ri,wateri   ;wait for data word
16              clr     ri          ;clear ri from data
17              setb    sm2         ;reset multiproc mode
18              mov     a,sbuf      ;read data
19              jz      datalo      ;jump if low data
20              setb    p1.7        ;set data bit high
21              sjmp    doneset     ;jump the clear
22  datalo:     clr     p1.7        ;data bit low
23  doneset:mov         a,p1        ;read switch
24              anl     a,#01h      ;mask other bits
25              mov     sbuf,a      ;transmit data
26              sjmp    notme       ;jump around clear
27  xmit:       clr     ti          ;clear xmit flag
28  notme:      pop     psw         ;see above
29              reti
30              end
```

FIGURE 6–10   *continued* (Slave 2)

sent. The slave then responds with a data byte showing the state of its switch. The master is, by this time, waiting for the data byte and uses the data to adjust the LED corresponding to slave #1. The process is then repeated for slave #2. During the communication of data bytes the unaddressed slave is unaffected, since its SM2 bit remains high.

This serial communications system can be expanded to 256 devices (an 8-bit address), but the driving capabilities of the microcontroller are limited and buffering would be needed to expand the system shown due to bus loading effects.

6–3   POWER CONTROL

Power control is important for embedded controllers, especially those used in battery-powered equipment. The CHMOS members of the 8051 family provide two levels of power control, idle mode and power-down mode. Both are invoked through software.

Idle mode is invoked by setting the IDL bit in the Power CONtrol (PCON) register. Since this register is not bit addressable, the usual way to accomplish this is by an ORL instruction. Idle mode shuts off the clock to the CPU, leaving the timers, interrupts, serial port, and RAM powered and working. All of the internal registers and memory retain their contents during idle-mode operation. Since the CPU accounts for about 85% of the power used, this represents a significant savings in spite of much of the chip remaining powered. Idle mode is terminated by either an interrupt (which must have been previously enabled) or by a system reset. If the 80C51 is awakened by an interrupt, the interrupt is run in the usual manner and then the program continues at the instruction immediately following the one that invoked the idle mode.

Power-down mode is invoked by setting the Power Down (PD) bit in PCON using an OR instruction as described above. Power-down mode freezes the system clock, preventing any parts of the system from running. In this way power-down mode can reduce the current further than idle mode. The bus drivers to port 2 are disabled during power-

```
1    sbit P1_6 = 0x96; /*define port bits*/
2    sbit P1_7 = 0x97;
3    #include <c:\c51\reg52.h>
4    #include <c:\c51\absacc.h>
5
6    void xmit (char mode, unsigned char datar)
7       {
8       if (mode == 1) TB8 = 1; /*set for addr. transmit*/
9       else TB8 = 0; /*set for data transmit*/
10      SBUF = datar; /*transmit*/
11      while (TI == 0); /*wait for ti to occur*/
12      TI = 0; /*clear ti*/
13      while (RI == 0); /*wait for transmission to be
                                       received*/
14      RI = 0; /*clear ri*/
15      }
16
17   main()
18      {
19      SCON = 0x98; /*9 bit UART, RCV enabled, TB8=1*/
20      while (1)
21         {
22         xmit(0x01,0x01); /*transmit addr. of slave 1*/
23         xmit(0x00,(P1 & 0x01)); /*transmit data*/
24         while (RI == 0); /*wait for return data*/
25         RI = 0; /*clear ri*/
26         if (SBUF == 0) P1_6 = 0; /*output data*/
27         else P1_6 = 1;
28         xmit(0x01,0x05); /*transmit addr. of slave 2*/
29         xmit(0x00,(P1 & 0x02)); /*transmit data*/
30         while (RI == 0); /*wait for return data*/
31         RI = 0; /*clear ri*/
32         if (SBUF == 0) P1_7 = 0; /*output data*/
33         else P1_7 = 1;
34         }
35
36      }
```

FIGURE 6–11 C-language multiprocessor software (Master).

```
1       sbit P1_7 = 0x97; /*define port bit*/
2       #include <c:\c51\reg52.h>
3       #include <c:\c51\absacc.h>
4
5       void ser()  interrupt 4 using 2
6          {
7         if (TI == 0)
8            {
9           RI = 0; /*clear ri*/
10          if (SBUF == 5) /*check address*/
11             {
12             SM2 = 0; /*clear multiproc mode*/
13             while (RI == 0); /*wait for data*/
14             RI = 0; /*clear ri*/
15             SM2 = 1; /*reset multiproc mode*/
16             if ((SBUF & 0x02) == 0x02) P1_7 = 1;
17             else P1_7 = 0; /*output data*/
18             SBUF = (P1 & 0x01); /*transmit data*/
19             }
20             }
21          else TI = 0; /*clear ti*/
22       }
23
24      main()
25         {
26         SCON = 0x0b0; /*9 bit UART, RCV enabled, sm2=1*/
27         IE = 0x90; /*enable serial interrupt*/
28         while (1);
29         }
```

FIGURE 6–11   *continued* (Slave 1)

down, and the contents of the port latch are asserted. Bits loaded into the port latch may be used to remove power from components external to the microcontroller for maximum power savings. Only a system reset will awaken a microcontroller in power-down mode. When it is awakened, the port bits are all set high by the reset and the processor restarts exactly as if power had been removed or a system reset had occurred. On-chip RAM and registers maintain their data during power-down, except those registers that are affected by a reset need to be reloaded to initialize peripherals such as timers, interrupts, and the serial port. Reset values for the SFRs are shown in Table 3–1.

Figure 6–12 shows a simple system that uses an nFET to control power to the memory and other devices during power-down mode. Only the processor and the reset capacitor are connected directly to VCC. For idle mode the nFET makes no difference, as it is not used. For power-down, however, the contents of the latches of port 2 become important. During normal operation using external memory, port 2 functions as the high byte of the address bus. The contents of the port 2 latches are not connected to the actual port pins that contain address information. During power-down operation the contents of the latches are actually driven out on the port pins and the address information is replaced by the contents of the latches. Therefore the contents of the latches must be set by software (writing data to port 2) before entering power-down mode. In the example shown, the latches are set so that P2.6 contains a 0 and P2.7 contains a 1. When power-down is

```
1       sbit P1_7 = 0x97; /*define port bit*/
2       #include <c:\c51\reg52.h>
3       #include <c:\c51\absacc.h>
4
5       void ser()  interrupt 4 using 2
6          {
7          if (TI == 0)
8             {
9             RI = 0; /*clear ri*/
10            if (SBUF == 5) /*check address*/
11               {
12               SM2 = 0; /*clear multiproc mode*/
13               while (RI == 0); /*wait for data*/
14               RI = 0; /*clear ri*/
15               SM2 = 1; /*reset multiproc mode*/
16               if ((SBUF & 0x02) == 0x02) P1_7 = 1;
17               else P1_7 = 0; /*output data*/
18               SBUF = (P1 & 0x01); /*transmit data*/
19               }
20            }
21         else TI = 0; /*clear ti*/
22      }
23
24      main()
25         {
26         SCON = 0x0b0; /*9 bit UART, RCV enabled, sm2=1*/
27         IE = 0x90; /*enable serial interrupt*/
28         while (1);
29         }
```

FIGURE 6–11   *continued* (Slave 2)

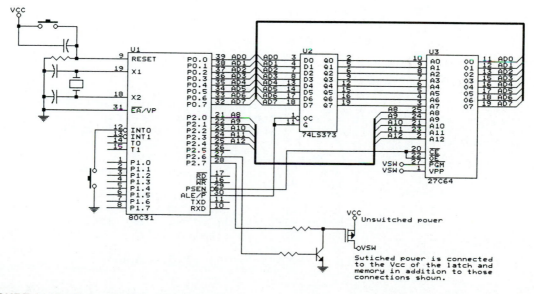

FIGURE 6–12   Power control example system.

```
1              org       2000h
2  start:      sjmp      init
3
4              org       0003h
5  serv0:      orl       pcon,#02h  ;set for power down
6              reti                 ;never used
7  init:       mov       ie,#81h    ;enable serial interrupt
8              mov       b,#100     ;5 second delay
9  delay:      mov       th0,#4ch   ;50 millisecs delay time
10             mov       tl0,#00h
11             clr       tf0        ;clear rollover flag
12             setb      tr0        ;turn on timer 0
13 tloop:      jnb       tf0,tloop  ;wait for rollover
14             clr       tr0        ;turn timer off
15             djnz      b,delay    ;loop until delay done
16             orl       pcon,#01h  ;set for idle mode
17             end
```

FIGURE 6–13 Assembly-language power control.

entered, the contents of the latches are asserted and the transistors switch off the power to the other chips. The only caution with this method of power control is that addresses that set the two control pins into the states mentioned above will also remove power to other chips.

Software to demonstrate both power control modes is shown in Figures 6–13 and 6–14. The programs work identically. They initialize the external 0 interrupt and then go into a 5-s wait period. During this period the current is about 35 mA. At the end of the

```
1   #include <c:\c51\reg52.h>
2
3   void ext0() interrupt 0 using 2
4     {
5     PCON = (PCON | 0x02);  /*power down mode*/
6     }
7
8   main()
9       {
10      unsigned char x; /*counter variable*/
11      IE = 0x81; /*enable serial interrupt*/
12      for (x=0; x<100; x++) /*5 second delay*/
13          {
14          TCON = 0x21; /*set up timer 0*/
15          TH0 = 0x4c; /* 50 millisecond delay */
16          TL0 = 0x00;
17          TF0 = 0;     /* clear rollover flag */
18          TR0 = 1;     /* turn timer on */
19          while (TF0 == 0); /* wait for roll over */
20          TR0 = 0;     /* timer off */
21          }
22      PCON = (PCON | 0x01); /*idle mode*/
23      }
```

FIGURE 6–14 C-language power control.

5-s period the processor enters idle mode by ORing PCON with 0x1 to set the IDL bit. The circuit shown draws about 8 mA in idle mode. The idle mode requires either an interrupt or a reset to awaken. In this case INT0 is enabled and so may be used to awaken the circuit. The interrupt service routine does nothing more than cause the processor to enter the power-down mode. This circuit draws about 100 μA while in power-down mode.

6-4 SUMMARY

The 8051 has five sources of interrupts, which may be enabled as desired by the programmer. The interrupts are attached to timer operation, serial communication, and external signals, and may be set to two levels of priority.

Many embedded controller projects must be battery powered. The power control features of the 8051 controllers allow two levels of power reduction.

Multiple 8051 processors may be interconnected using a single serial communication link. The communication facilities of the 8051 provide a convenient method of controlling multiple processors.

6-5 EXERCISES

1. Determine the necessary contents for IP and IE to provide the following conditions:
    a. Enable only the interrupts for the serial port and for timer 0, giving timer 0 priority.
    b. Enable both timer interrupts, giving both low priority.
    c. Enable only the external interrupt 1 and serial interrupts. The external interrupt must be edge triggered and able to interrupt the serial interrupt.
2. Modify Figure 6–9 to add a third slave whose address must be 7.

CHAPTER 7

Project Development

OVERVIEW

This chapter provides insight into the development cycle of microprocessor-based projects. Included are the general steps in project development and three example projects to illustrate the broad application of the 8051 family of microcontrollers. The first of the examples, an avian incubator, is covered in great detail to illustrate the process of project development. The balance of the projects are covered in a more concise manner.

The success of the original 8051 family of microcontrollers has spawned a wide range of descendants. For the most part the descendants have come about in order to enhance the original family. Descendant microcontrollers that add particularly interesting additions to the 8051 family are also explored. A major aspect to any project is the choice of the ''best'' microcontroller to complete the project. Where appropriate, these descendent processors are applied to projects.

7-1   THE 8052 FAMILY

The first of the descendants is the 8052 family of microcontrollers. The 8052 was an attempt to increase the processing power of the 8051 through the addition of memory and an additional timer. These parts were produced by Intel and have since been second-sourced by several vendors.

The 8052 processors (8032, 80C32, 8052, 80C52, 87C52, etc.) are virtually identical to the 8051 family and are code-compatible in all respects. The additions that separate the 8052 family are an additional 4K of code space (8K total), another 128 bytes of internal RAM, and a third timer/counter.

The code space works exactly as in the 8051 except that with EA high the processor looks internally for code when the address is below 0x2000. Above that address the processor looks in external code space for its program. As with the basic 8051 family processors, pulling EA low forces the processor to look in external code space for its program.

The additional internal RAM occupies the same internal addresses as the SFRs. It is addressed using indirect addressing techniques. Direct addressing is still used to address the SFRs. In other words, the addressing method determines whether the upper 128 bytes of memory or the SFRs are being accessed.

The third timer, T2, is a flexible counter/timer unit that is somewhat different than T0 and T1. T2 can be used as either a counter or a timer, like T0 and T1, but it has additional features. Figure 7–1 shows the bit definitions for SFR T2CON, the Timer 2 CONtrol Register. This timer operates in either capture mode or reload mode, with the mode controlled by the CP/RL2\ bit in T2CON.

Capture mode, shown in Figure 7–2, is designed to allow an external hardware event to capture the count when the event occurs and to generate an interrupt at the same time. For this to work, the C/$\overline{T2}$ and EXEN2 bits must be set to enable the edge detector output, which causes a capture and an interrupt. Capture mode might be used to measure a frequency. Whenever the external frequency causes a falling edge at the T2EX pin, the count is captured and an interrupt is generated. At this point the interrupt service routine (at vector address 0x002b) reads the capture registers, and by subtracting the previous reading from the current reading, determines the time between edges and the frequency.

As shown in Figure 7–3, reload mode is similar to mode 2 of timers 0 and 1 except that T2 is always a 16-bit reloadable counter. Consequently, it is capable of greater divisions in the reload mode than T0 or T1. Reload mode is established whenever C/$\overline{T2}$ is cleared. Reload takes place whenever rollover occurs, and an interrupt is generated if the ET2 bit (IE bit 5) is set. If the EXEN2 bit is set, a reload (and an interrupt) may also

TF2	EXF2	RCLK	TCLK	EXEN2	TR2	C/T2\	CP/RL2\

CP/RL2\	Capture/Reload Flag. Set for capture mode and cleared for reload mode.
C/T2\	Counter/Timer control bit. Set for external event counter, cleared for internal oscillator.
TR2	Timer 2 Run bit. Set for run, cleared for stop.
EXEN2	Timer 2 External Enable Flag. Set to allow a negative edge at T2EX to cause reload or capture. Clear to disable inputs at T2EX.
TCLK	Transmit Clock Flag. Set to use T2 as the transmit baud rate clock. Clear to use T1 as the baud rate clock for transmit.
RCLK	Receive Clock Flag. Set to use T2 as the receive baud rate clock, clear to use T1 as the baud rate clock for receive.
EXF2	External Flag. Set when capture or reload is caused by a negative edge on T2EX and when EXEN2 is set.
TF2	Timer 2 Overflow Flag. Set when T2 rolls over from ones to zeros. Will not be set if RCLK or TCLK is set.

FIGURE 7–1 T2CON bit definitions.

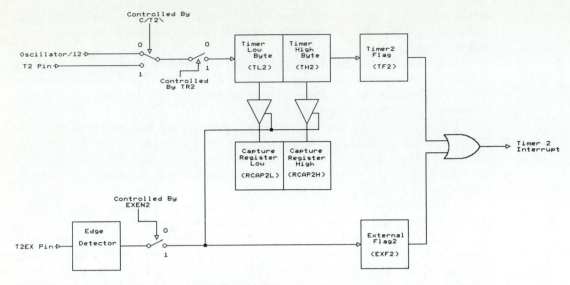

FIGURE 7–2   Timer 2 capture mode block diagram.

be triggered by a falling edge at T2EX. This mode is useful for generating an output frequency or for generating a time base for microcontroller operations as discussed in Chapter 6.

As shown in Figure 7–4, T2 can be configured in a mode similar to reload mode to provide baud rate clocks for the serial port. This mode is established by clearing

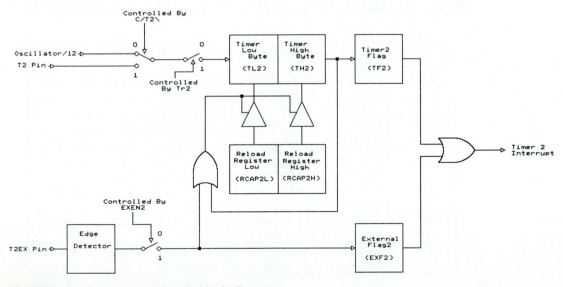

FIGURE 7–3   Timer 2 reload mode block diagram.

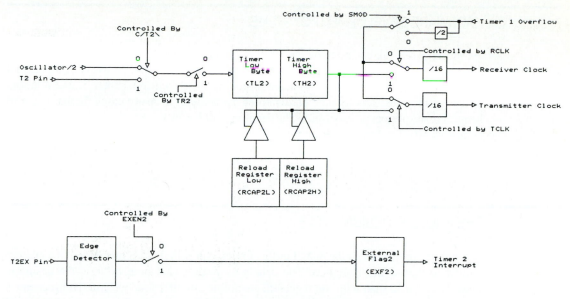

FIGURE 7–4 Timer 2 baud rate generator mode block diagram.

$C/\overline{T2}$ and setting either RCLK or TCLK or both. In this mode the reload occurs whenever rollover occurs, and the rollover frequency is then divided by 16 to become the baud rate clock(s). Note that timer 2 is driven by the oscillator frequency divided by 2 (not 12) in this mode. RCLK and TCLK determine which of the serial port options is driven by T2. The baud rate in serial port modes 1 and 3 is determined by

$$\text{Serial baud rate} = \frac{\text{timer 2 overflow rate}}{16}$$

The timer 2 interrupt, if enabled in IE, continues to function in the usual manner provided that EXEN2 is set. It may be used as an additional external interrupt.

7–2 THE 80C552 MICROCONTROLLERS

The 80C552 family of microcontrollers is typical of the microcontrollers expanded from the 8051 family. These devices remain code-compatible but greatly expand the functions of the device. The 80C552 contains the 8052 core and also includes a total of six parallel ports, two PWM output channels, a watchdog timer, and eight channels of A/D (10-bit resolution). More details relative to the 80C552 devices are given in the project sections that follow.

7–3   ## HARDWARE DEVELOPMENT SYSTEMS

Hardware development systems are used to simplify the process of creating working microcontroller systems. A hardware development system usually consists of a personal computer (PC), a software development system as described in Chapter 3, and a means to try out the programs and the hardware of the project. In many cases the hardware to be used in the project is also used as the development hardware. In other cases a standalone computer board is interfaced to the project hardware for tryout. Hardware development systems are discussed further in the next section.

7–4   ## THE PROJECT DESIGN CYCLE

Designing a project using the 8051 family of microcontrollers is accomplished in a manner similar to that of most projects. The details vary somewhat both because the design is more constrained than with more general electronic circuitry and because the processor's computational power leaves more opportunities for trade-offs between hardware and software.

The steps for project design are:

1. Define the scope of the project.
2. Design/plan the hardware and software.
3. Build and test the hardware.
4. Write and test the software.
5. Test the system operationally.

Defining the scope of the project involves determining exactly what the end project will do and how it will do it. One of the products of step 1 is a list of specifications and features. The other is a basic block diagram, which is refined into a detailed block diagram in step 2.

Step 2 involves expansion of the basic block diagram from step 1. The block diagram is expanded and detailed until it eventually becomes the schematic for the device. Step 2 includes definition of all of the interblock signals and definition of software modules and their tasks. At the conclusion of this phase, the appearance of all displays, the nature of all inputs, the signal requirements for each block, and the structure of the software are known. A large project can at this point be broken into several smaller projects (which may be completed by different people), because the definitions are complete and each block may be treated independently.

Step 3 is to design, build, and test the hardware. The goal of this step is to test each block of the project by itself and then test it with the microcontroller.

Step 4 is to develop working software that will run the project in its entirety. The software is developed in a modular fashion, as the hardware was in step 3. Software in the form of subroutines or functions is developed that will interface with each block of the project. As each subroutine or function is developed, it is tested independently. With the hardware known to be functional, any problems found are isolated to the software module being developed, so the developer is spared the agony of hunting through both the hardware and the entire program wondering where the problem lies.

Step 5 is to test the entire project operationally. Often it is necessary to run a project for a period of time to assure that all aspects of the project work as intended.

7–5   ## AN INCUBATOR PROJECT

Define the Scope of the Project

This project is to produce an incubator for raising small birds. Bird babies are often removed from the mother when they first hatch, so that they will be more gentle and acclimated to people. The babies require a temperature of about 105°F, which is gradually reduced to room temperature as the babies acquire feathers.

Microcontrollers are well suited to these types of control applications, and although the incubator could probably be controlled without the use of a microcontroller, using one will allow more convenience and ''user friendliness'' than might otherwise be possible.

Whether the project is assigned by a supervisor in an industrial situation, or whether the project is for your next-door neighbor who raises birds, it should be completed in very much the same manner. Specifically, it is necessary to establish the end result of the project in an explicit manner. In the case of the incubator, it is important to define its operation and specifications before proceeding. Given the operating guidelines and specifications, it is then possible to create a very basic block diagram for the project. Step 1 is completed once the basic block diagram is done.

In the case of the incubator, the following are given by whoever is asking for the device: It must work in an inexpensive, small-size drink cooler from a discount store. It must maintain the temperature within ±0.5°F of the set temperature. There must be a way to adjust the desired temperature accurately, and the device should display the current temperature accurately to 0.1°F. The device should also consume as little current as possible, because the person who wants the project plans to run it on batteries at some point in the future.

At this point it is desirable to codify the specifications for review by the person who wants the project. To wit:

Bird Incubator

Maintains temperature ±0.5°F in the range 70–110°F in a small cooler

Provides a means to adjust set-point temperature

Displays set point while setting the temperature and operating temperature at all other times

Minimizes current drain

In the normal course of a project such as this one, it would be necessary to investigate the thermal properties of the cooler, the mechanics of assuring even heat in the incubator, and so forth. For this project we will assume that all this study has been done and an appropriate heating scheme is to use a flat plate of $\frac{1}{8}$-in. aluminum in the bottom of the cooler. Attached to the plate will be a 10-W wire-wound resistor to provide the heat and a temperature sensor to provide temperature measurement.

With all of the mechanical details taken care of, it is possible to construct a basic block diagram simply by thinking about the nature of the project. The temperature must be read by the microcontroller and used to adjust the heat. In addition, the temperature needs to be displayed and a means provided to adjust the set point. The temperature sensor and the heater are analog devices, and so some form of analog-to-digital and digital-to-analog conversion will be needed as interfaces to the microcontroller. A display capable of displaying at least four digits will be required, and some controls will be needed.

The basic block diagram in Figure 7–5 shows the overall flow of signals through the project. In this case the incubator is at the bottom. The temperature signal flows from the sensor to the analog interface, where it is converted to digital and then sent to the microcontroller. The microcontroller is responsible for the output of the digital control signals to the analog interface, which converts them into appropriate analog signals to drive the heater. In addition, the microcontroller reads the controls and outputs information to the display.

Step 1 of the project development process is complete. An overall picture exists of the functions and control circuitry needed. The important point to see in the basic block diagram is that *no* decisions have been made as to *how* any of the blocks will work. The decisions as to how the blocks work are made in step 2.

FIGURE 7–5   Basic incubator block diagram.

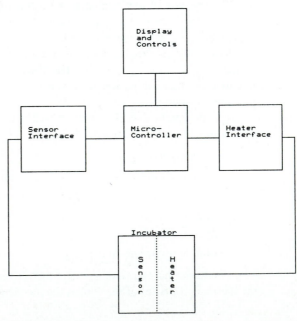

Design/Plan the Hardware and Software

Step 2 is usually the longest of the steps in terms of time and effort. The block diagram must be developed into a tentative schematic and the hardware/software development system established.

Before the block diagram can be refined further, decisions are required as to how the project will operate. An operating method for each block of the diagram must be determined on a block-by-block basis. First, alternatives for each block are determined, and then a choice is made for each block.

The first of the blocks considered is usually the operator interface. In this case the operator interface consists of the control panel and display. The major concern with the operator interface is that it be simple and easy to work. The term "user friendly" definitely applies here. Alternatives for this interface should be developed for evaluation. Some of the alternatives for the incubator (keeping in mind that the operator needs to be able to read the temperature during operation, and to be able to set the desired temperature) are:

Using a dipswitch in conjunction with a printed table of settings to set the desired operating temperature. Advantages: low cost, simple interface. Disadvantages: cumbersome and tricky for the operator to use.

Using a potentiometer to set the desired temperature. Advantages: simple to use, reasonably priced. Disadvantages: another analog device to interface to the controller. Also requires some method to put the microcontroller into a "set" mode so it knows when to read the potentiometer.

Using three pushbuttons in a manner similar to an alarm clock (hold one button down while setting, the other two buttons being to raise or lower the set point). Advantages: very inexpensive, a very simple electronic interface, and a familiar operator interface for most folks. Disadvantages: requires more software (most people will expect to be able to hold the button down to raise or lower the set-point temperature continuously).

Use seven-segment LED digit displays. Advantages: bright and easily readable. Disadvantages: require significant amounts of current, relatively complex interface, and more software.

Use an LCD interface as described in Chapter 5. Advantages: simple software and electronic interface. Disadvantage: relatively high cost.

Use an LCD four-digit numeric display, which requires a three-wire serial digital interface. Advantages: simple electronic interface, large and easy to read, relatively inexpensive. Disadvantage: able to display only digits.

The list of alternatives clearly demonstrates that more than one method exists to accomplish almost any task. There are in fact many more possible choices for this project besides those shown in the list. Selecting from among the alternatives is an important part of step 2 of the development process. For the incubator, the "alarm clock" control panel and numeric LCD seem to be the best balance between cost and ease of use.

The next logical block to consider is the input block. In this case the inputs consist of the temperature sensor and A/D conversion interface. The criteria for the temperature sensor and A/D conversion block are that they must provide measurement of the required temperature range and a digital signal for the microcontroller that is a linear function of temperature at an acceptable resolution. The incubator is to control temperature to 0.5°F and display it to 0.1°F. The range of temperature to be displayed/controlled is 70–110°F. The range is 40° (110 − 70). A good rule of thumb for control is to be able to measure/ control to a level 10 times better than required. The incubator is to be controlled ±0.5°F. Ten times better would be 0.05°F. The actual resolution required is then 40/0.05 resolution or 800 steps. This requires an A/D conversion resolution of 10 bits (1024 steps) to perform adequately. The actual resolution is then $40/2^{10} - 1$ or 0.039°F.

For the display it would be desirable to show the results to 0.01°F (10 times better than 0.1°F), which would require 4000 steps. A 12-bit converter would be required to achieve this resolution. A 12-bit conversion scheme adds more cost and complexity for what is only a cosmetic improvement.

Alternatives for these blocks might include:

A thermocouple or thermistor connected into a resistive bridge. The output from this circuit could be fed to an A/D conversion. Advantage: simple circuit. Disadvantages: questionable linearity and critical bridge component tolerances.

A solid-state temperature sensor such as the National LM335. Advantage: the output is linear and absolute with respect to temperature. Disadvantage: none.

An A/D converter as discussed in Chapter 5. Advantage: inexpensive. Disadvantages: requires 10 data lines plus two or three control lines from the microcontroller (complex interface) as well as a clock.

A voltage-to-frequency converter to output a frequency proportional to the temperature. Advantages: simple circuitry, adequate linearity. Disadvantage: complexity of software to measure frequency.

The National LM335 temperature sensor is chosen to offer the best linearity at minimum expense. The choices for the A/D are not so easy. A frequency-to-voltage converter such as the National LM331 could be used as the converter for this circuit, provided that the requirements for linearity and resolution are met. In this instance, an A/D converter is chosen for simplicity of development. An AD573 is an appropriate choice. The AD573 is a 10-bit converter with a simple interface.

The LM335 temperature sensor outputs 10 mV per degree kelvin (0°C = 273 K). Table 7–1 shows the output from the sensor at the relevant temperatures. The sensor will output a range of 2.94 to 3.16 V for the temperature range of the incubator. Unfortunately, the resolution of the controller was calculated assuming a full-scale voltage into the A/D converter. There is, then, a basic problem between stages of the project: The sensor outputs 2.94 to 3.16 V to feed a converter expecting a 0- to 10-V input. The zero and span circuit shown in Figure 7–6 interfaces the temperature sensor to the A/D by modifying

TABLE 7–1 Temperature sensor voltage

Temp. (°F)	Temp. (°C)	Temp. (K)	Sensor Voltage
70	21.1	294.1	2.94V
110	43.3	316.3	3.16V

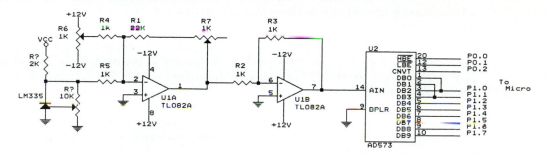

FIGURE 7–6   Temperature measurement circuit.

the 2.94 to 3.16 signal from the sensor to a 0- to 10-V signal for the A/D. The complete temperature measurement block is shown in Figure 7–6.

The input signal is now correctly interfaced to the A/D converter and, since the inputs and outputs of the A/D converter are TTL-level signals, the A/D will interface directly to the microcontroller. Given the interface and temperature range, a value of 0000000000_2 represents a temperature of 70°F and a value of 1111111111_2 represents a temperature of 110°F.

The final choice relative to the input blocks is how to represent the temperature internally to the microcontroller. The only two real choices for representing the temperature are as degrees or as the raw data from the A/D. This project uses the raw data from the A/D for internal control purposes.

The last block to be developed is the output driver for the heater. This block must convert the digital information from the microcontroller into an analog signal with sufficient power to drive the heater. The alternatives are:

> Convert a digital word (8 bits) into an analog voltage to provide heat. In this instance a D/A could be used, which would, in turn, drive a power output stage to control the voltage to the heater (resistor) linearly. Advantage: relatively straightforward. Disadvantages: uses several parts, dissipates heat in the power driver.

> Use a PWM driver as the analog converter. Advantages: simpler circuit, no power dissipated in driver. Disadvantage: more complex programming.

The second alternative is seemingly the best for this project in spite of the complexity of the software. The simplest implementation of this block is to use an FET to switch the power to the heater. Figure 7–7 shows such a driver.

FIGURE 7–7   Pulse-width
heater driver.

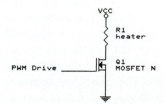

The decisions made previously determine the amount of I/O needed by the microcontroller, which will in turn affect the choice of microcontroller for the project. The balance of the project is now defined, and the microcontroller must be chosen. The 8051 microcontrollers are the subject of this book, but they are not the only microcontrollers available. Each project needs to use the microcontroller that best fits the project.

Choice of a microcontroller depends on the amount of I/O needed, the processing power needed, and the size of the code and data storage needed. The I/O requirements are (as determined previously):

A/D converter:	8 bits for data
	3 lines for control
Display:	3 lines
Controls:	3 lines
Output:	1 line

The task for this project is to control the temperature and adjust the output drive to maintain the desired heat. The microcontroller needs to provide PWM drive controlled by the temperature input. Occasionally, the controls need to be read to adjust the set point. These tasks do not need large amounts of code or data storage. These requirements lead to the following microcontroller alternatives:

80C51

87C51

87C52

80C552

87C751

All of the processors shown have adequate processing power for the job. CMOS versions are being considered in order to meet the power consumption requirements. Refer to the appropriate manufacturers' literature for more details about each (the latter two parts are made by Signetics). The 80C51 requires an external ROM to hold the program code, leaving only 15 lines for I/O. This rules it out. The 87C51 and 87C52 provide internal EPROM for program storage, leaving all 32 I/O lines free. These microcontrollers would meet the requirements of the project. The 87C52 has more memory than is required for the job, and is probably not a good choice as it would be overkill for the job. The 87C51, then, appears to be a good choice to meet the hardware requirements. Looking a bit further, the 87C51 provides more than adequate I/O, provides software PWM, and is capable of the task.

The 80C552 is listed as an alternative because it has built-in automatic PWM. It also has six I/O ports and built-in A/D conversion. This makes it also overqualified for the project, but serves to point out the large variety of built-in peripherals available in members of the 8051 family. The built-in peripherals may reduce the amount of circuitry in the project, but they do require external memory.

The 87C751 is another relative of the 8051 family. It is a physically smaller cousin to the 8051. The entire core microcontroller is included, but the ability to use external memory is missing (internal code memory is provided) and only 19 I/O lines are available.

Allowing for external A/D circuitry, the 87C751 is an adequate choice for this project. In fact, given the size and power constraints, it is actually the best choice.

The final choice to be made is the development system. The 87C751 microcontroller uses only internal memory for program storage, making it difficult to use for project development. Parts are available with either EPROM (higher cost) or one-time-programmable program storage. Neither of these is convenient for program development. In this instance it is probably better to use an 8051-based single board for development and move the program to an 87C751 after it is working.

The 87C751 microcontroller is shown in Figure 7–8.

Step 2 is now complete, with tentative schematics, development system, and operating scheme ready for further development.

Build and Test the Hardware

Step 3 has as its major purpose to assure that the hardware is correct before beginning software development. The tentative schematics are reduced to working circuits.

Beginning with the controls and display, each circuit is built and tested. The controls are simple pushbuttons connected as shown in Figure 7–9. The push-button switches are connected to provide a logic low when pressed. Testing them involves only using a measuring device to assure that the proper levels show up at the microcontroller's pins when the buttons are pressed.

The display is somewhat more difficult to test. It requires a serial bit stream and clock to load data into the display. Specifically, the display requires a serial bit stream of 32 bits (8 bits per digit × 4 digits). The 8 bits per digit are made up of 1 bit for each of the seven segments and 1 bit for the decimal point associated with each digit.

The bits are in the following order relative to the segments:

g f a b c d e dp

As shown, the "dp" bit is clocked in first, then the bit for segment "e," and so on. The stream is repeated four times, once for each digit, to make up the entire 32-bit data stream. After clocking in the entire data stream, the load pin is pulsed high to load the new data into the display.

Testing the display is accomplished with two debounced pushbuttons and a switch to set the input data either high or low. Set the switch to the value of the LSB of one of

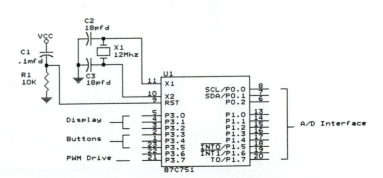

FIGURE 7–8 87C751 micro-controller.

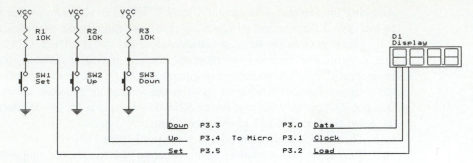

FIGURE 7–9   User interface.

the numeric digits, and toggle the clock once. Then set the switch to the second bit value and provide another clock pulse, continuing until all 8 bits have been clocked into the display. Finally, toggle the load pin once to see the results. The number chosen will appear in the first position of the display. Table 7–2 shows the bit patterns required to display each of the 10 numeric digits.

Now that the display and controls have been tested, the output stage may be built and tested. The circuit is assembled per the tentative schematic and a large value (as compared to the 10-W heater resistor) is put in place of the heater resistor. Using V_{cc} to power the heater would require 2 A from the power supply to provide the 10 W for heat. It would also cause the regulator to dissipate additional power. In all likelihood the V_{cc} for the circuitry will be regulated down from a higher battery voltage such as 12 V. It is a more efficient design to use the unregulated voltage for the high-power portions of the circuit. Assuming an unregulated voltage of 12 V, the heater resistor is $R = [(12 \text{ V})^2/10 \text{ W}] = 14.4 \ \Omega \approx 15 \ \Omega$. A resistor of about 500 Ω is used for test purposes to limit the current.

After connecting the circuit, the voltage across the test resistor is monitored while applying a logic 0 and a logic 1 to the gate. The logic 0 causes no voltage to appear on the test resistor, and the logic 1 causes the full 12 V (minus ≈ 0.1 V) to appear on the

TABLE 7–2   Display codes

Digit	g	f	a	b	c	d	e	dp	Hex Code
0	0	1	1	1	1	1	1	0	0x7E
1	0	0	0	1	1	0	0	0	0x18
2	1	0	1	1	0	1	1	0	0xB6
3	1	0	1	1	1	1	0	0	0xBC
4	1	1	0	1	1	0	0	0	0xD8
5	1	1	1	0	1	1	0	0	0xEC
6	1	1	1	0	1	1	1	0	0xEE
7	0	0	1	1	1	0	0	0	0x38
8	1	1	1	1	1	1	1	0	0xFE
9	1	1	1	1	1	1	0	0	0xFC

test resistor. Following this test, the real 10-W heater may be connected into the circuit for a final test of the heater.

Next, the temperature measurement block is implemented. The block is composed of three distinct parts: the temperature sensor, the zero-and-span circuit, and the A/D. Each is developed and tested individually.

The temperature sensor may be wired up and calibrated by attaching a voltmeter to its output, calculating the theoretical output for the temperature of the room in which the work is being done, and adjusting the potentiometer for the correct output.

The zero-and-span circuit is tested similarly. The circuit is wired with a potentiometer attached to the input in place of the sensor. Adjusting the potentiometer to output 2.94 V (simulating a temperature of 70°F—refer to Table 7–1), the output may be adjusted to 0 V using R6. Similarly, inputting a voltage of 3.16 V, R7 may be adjusted so that the circuit outputs 10 V. These two adjustments interact to some extent and need to be repeated until no further adjustments are required.

Last, the A/D is assembled and tested. A voltage source of 0–10 V is used to test the A/D by setting the analog input and observing the binary output. The conversion is begun by creating a positive pulse on the convert pin. After allowing a few microseconds for the conversion to finish, the $\overline{HBE}$ and $\overline{LBE}$ are driven low one at a time to output the high byte and low byte, respectively.

The hardware is complete and the project now moves into software development.

Write and Test the Software

Developing software proceeds in a step-by-step manner much like hardware development. Each module of the project software is created and tested independently before assembling the modules into the final program.

The first module is the display driver. Developing this module allows the display to be used while testing the subsequent modules. The display module has two purposes: to translate the digits to be displayed into the bits streams for each digit and to serially shift the streams into the display.

The modules utilize a table to translate the data into the bit streams and then the programs shift out the bit streams as required for the display. The modules also blank the first (MS) digit if it is 0, for a more pleasing display. The software modules are shown in Figures 7–10 and 7–11.

The two programs work identically. The "init" or "main" functions set up a number to be displayed and initialize the load and clock lines to the display. They then call the "dispnum" function to display the digits. "Dispnum" converts the digit to a display code, blanks the first digit if it is a 0, adds in the decimal to the least significant digit, and serially shifts the digit out on the data line with appropriate clock pulses. Finally, the load line is toggled to cause the new information to be displayed.

These programs are examples of the use of modular program development. The important module ("dispnum" in this case) is created along with just enough code in the main program loop to exercise the module. Reassembling or recompiling with different numbers to be displayed allows testing all 10 digits. The module thus developed is kept for final use while the main code is changed as needed to test additional modules. In this way the modules are developed and kept for use in the final program.

```
1           ;Display driver module
2           disport equ      0b0h                    ;port 3 is display
3
4                   org       2000h
5           start:  ljmp      init                    ;jump to init
6
7           dispnum:mov       dptr,#disptab           ;point to conv. table
8                   mov       r0,#20h                 ;point to LS digit
9           displp: mov       a,@r0                   ;get first digit
10                  cjne      r0,#23h,notfour         ;jump if not MSD
11                  cjne      a,#0,notfour            ;jump if LSD not zero
12                  mov       a,#0ah                  ;set blanking code
13          notfour:movc      a,@a+dptr               ;get display code
14                  cjne      r0,#20h,notfrst         ;jump if not LS digit
15                  orl       a,#01                   ;decimal on if LSD 16
16          notfrst:mov       r4,#8                   ;display 8 bits
17          xlp:    rrc       a                       ;rotate bit to C
18                  mov       disport.0,c             ;bit to data port
19                  clr       disport.1               ;make clock
20                  setb      disport.1
21                  djnz      r4,xlp                  ;finished 8 bits yet?
22                  inc       r0                      ;bump pointer
23                  cjne      r0,#24h,displp          ;repeat if not done
24                  setb      disport.2               ;toggle load line
25                  clr       disport.2
26                  ret
27
28          disptab:db        07eh,018h,0b6h,0bch,0d8h ;0,1,2,3,4
29                  db        0ech,0eeh,038h,0feh,0fch ;5,6,7,8,9
30                  db        000h                            ;blank
31
32          init:   clr       disport.2               ;preset load line
33                  setb      disport.1               ;preset clock line
34                  mov       20h,#6                  ;first (LS) digit
35                  mov       21h,#8                  ;second digit
36                  mov       22h,#9                  ;third digit
37                  mov       23h,#0                  ;fourth digit
38                  acall     dispnum                 ;display'em
39                  ljmp      0030h                   ;exit
40
41                  end
```

FIGURE 7-10 Assembly language display test.

The next module to be developed is the module to convert a raw number (0 to 0x3ff) into displayable digits in the range of 70 to 110°F. The purpose of doing this module now is to provide a convenient means to test the controls and A/D.

The problem here is one of mathematics. Seventy is to be displayed when the raw data number is 0, and 110 is to be displayed when the raw data is 0x3ff. This is especially difficult in assembly language, where only integer math is possible and the display is to show increments of 0.1°F. In this case the program displays and works with values of 700 to 1100 (10 times the actual value). The dispnum routine will automatically add in the decimal point.

The formula for the conversion is:

$$\text{display value} = \text{raw data} * (1100 - 700)/1024 + 700$$

$$= \text{raw data} * 25/64 + 700$$

The final form can be double precision in assembly language, although no 16-bit math instructions are included in the 8051 family instruction set. The math operations

```
1    #include <reg552.h>
2
3    extern void gomon(); /*return to monitor prog.*/
4
5    unsigned char DISPDIGS[4]; /*array to hold digits*/
6    sbit DDATA = 0xb0;  /*data bit*/
7    sbit CLK=0xb1;    /*clock bit*/
8    sbit LOAD=0xb2;   /*load bit*/
9
10   unsigned char DISTAB [] = {0x7e,0x18,0xb6,0xbc,0xd8,
11                              0xec,0xee,0x38,0xfe,0xfc,
12                              0x00};
13   void dispnum(void)
14       {
15       unsigned char cntr, digit, bitcntr;
16                 /*counter, digit, bit counter*/
17       if (DISPDIGS[3] == 0) DISPDIGS[3]=0xa;
18                 /*blank if MSD = 0*/
19       for (cntr=0; cntr<4; cntr++)
20           {
21           digit = DISTAB[DISPDIGS[cntr]];
22           if (cntr == 0) digit = (digit | 0x01);
23                     /*decimal on if LSD*/
24           for (bitcntr=0; bitcntr<8; bitcntr++)
25               {
26               DDATA = (digit & 0x01);   /*output data bit*/
27               CLK = 0;     /*make clock*/
28               CLK = 1;
29               digit = (digit >> 1); /*shift bit*/
30               }
31           }
32       LOAD = 1;   /*load pulse*/
33       LOAD = 0;
34       }
35
36   main()
37       {
38       unsigned char q;
39       CLK = 1;   /*preset clock*/
40       LOAD = 0; /*preset load*/
41       DISPDIGS[0]=6;   /*load array*/
42       DISPDIGS[1]=8;   /*load array*/
43       DISPDIGS[2]=9;   /*load array*/
44       DISPDIGS[3]=0;   /*load array*/
45       dispnum();     /*display digits*/
46       gomon();   /*return to monitor*/
47       }
```

FIGURE 7-11 C-Language display test.

```
1          ;Display driver module
2          disport equ      0b0h                 ;display port
3
4                  org      2000h
5          start:  ljmp     init                 ;jump to init
6
7          dispnum:mov      dptr,#disptab        ;point to conv. table
8                  mov      r0,#20h              ;point to LS digit
9          displp: mov      a,@r0                ;get first digit
10                 cjne     r0,#23h,notfour      ;jump if not MSD
11                 cjne     a,#0,notfour         ;jump if not zero
12                 mov      a,#0ah               ;set blanking code
13         notfour:movc     a,@a+dptr            ;get display code
14                 cjne     r0,#20h,notfrst      ;jump if not LS digit
15                 orl      a,#01                ;light decimal
16         notfrst:mov      r4,#8                ;display 8 bits
17         xlp:    rrc      a                    ;rotate bit to C
18                 mov      disport.0,c          ;bit to data port
19                 clr      disport.1            ;make clock
20                 setb     disport.1
21                 djnz     r4,xlp               ;finished 8 bits yet?
22                 inc      r0                   ;bump pointer
23                 cjne     r0,#24h,displp       ;repeat if not done
24                 setb     disport.2            ;toggle load line
25                 clr      disport.2
26                 ret
27
28         disptab:db       07eh,018h,0b6h,0bch,0d8h ;0,1,2,3,4
29                 db       0ech,0eeh,038h,0feh,0fch ;5,6,7,8,9
30                 db       000h                     ;blank
31
32         cnvrt:  mov      b,#25                ;multipy by 25
33                 mov      a,r0                 ;lo byte first
34                 mul      ab                   ;multiply lo byte
35                 mov      r2,a                 ;save lo result
36                 mov      r3,b                 ;save high result
37                 mov      b,#25                ;multiply high byte
38                 mov      a,r1                 ;get high byte
39                 mul      ab                   ;multiply it
40                 add      a,r3                 ;add 1st high byte
41         ;results now in a(high byte) and r2 (low byte)
42         ;need to divide by 64 by shifting 6 bits right
43                 rl       a                    ;reorder bits
44                 rl       a
45                 push     acc                  ;save bits
46                 anl      a,#3h                ;get highest byte
47                 mov      r5,a                 ;save it
48                 pop      acc                  ;recover bits
49                 anl      a,#0fch              ;mask lower byte
50                 mov      r3,a                 ;save it
51                 mov      a,r2                 ;get low byte
52                 rl       a                    ;repeat
53                 rl       a
54                 anl      a,#03h               ;mask unwanted bits
```

FIGURE 7–12 Digit conversion module in assembly.

```
55                orl       a,r3              ;complete division
56        ;results now high byte in r5 low byte in acc
57        ;now add 700 (2bch hex)
58                add       a,#0bch           ;add low part
59                mov       dpl,a             ;save it
60                mov       a,r5              ;get high byte
61                addc      a,#02h            ;get high result
62                mov       dph,a             ;result in dptr
63        ;math done results are in the dptr
64        ;now need to extract the digits for dispnum
65                mov       20h,#0            ;clear digit counters
66                mov       21h,#0            ;10's digit
67                mov       22h,#0            ;100's digit
68                mov       23h,#0            ;1000's digit
69        cntlp:  mov       a,dpl             ;get low byte
70                orl       a,dph             ;or in high byte
71                jz        donecnt           ;jump if finished
72                dec       dpl               ;decr count
73                mov       a,dpl             ;get count byte
74                cjne      a,#0ffh,noroll    ;check for rollover
75                dec       dph               ;decr high byte
76        noroll: inc       20h               ;incr ones
77                mov       a,20h             ;check for rollover
78                cjne      a,#10,cntlp       ;jump if no roll
79                mov       20h,#0            ;clear ones
80                inc       21h               ;incr tens
81                mov       a,21h             ;get tens
82                cjne      a,#10,cntlp       ;check for rollover
83                mov       21h,#0            ;clear tens
84                inc       22h               ;incr hundreds
85                mov       a,22h             ;get hundreds
86                cjne      a,#10,cntlp       ;check for rollover
87                mov       22h,#0            ;clear hundreds
88                inc       23h               ;incr thousands
89                sjmp      cntlp
90        donecnt:acall     dispnum           ;convert and display
91                ret
92
93        init:   clr       disport.2         ;preset load line
94                setb      disport.1         ;preset clock line
95                mov       r0,#00h           ;data(0x200=90deg)
96                mov       r1,#02h           ;MS byte
97                acall     cnvrt             ;convert/display data
98                ljmp      0030h             ;exit
99
100               end
```

FIGURE 7–12 *continued*

are therefore done through software. Following the math conversion, the digits are extracted by a series of divisions and subtractions. The resulting digits are displayed via dispnum for test purposes. The programs are shown in Figures 7–12 and 7–13.

These two programs implement the formula given above and send the results to the dispnum module. The result is that the test data is displayed in the form of degrees

```
1       #include <reg552.h>
2
3
4       extern void gomon();
5
6       unsigned char DISPDIGS[4]; /*digits array*/
7       sbit DDATA = 0xb0;   /*data bit*/
8       sbit CLK=0xc1;     /*clock bit*/
9       sbit LOAD=0xc2;    /*load bit*/
10
11      unsigned char DISTAB [] = {0x7e,0x18,0xb6,0xbc,0xd8,
12                                 0xec,0xee,0x38,0xfe,0xfc,
13                                 0x00};
14      void dispnum(void)
15          {
16          unsigned char cntr, digit, bitcntr;
17                   /*counter, digit, bit counter*/
18          if (DISPDIGS[3] == 0) DISPDIGS[3]=0xa;
19                   /*blank if MSD = 0*/
20          for (cntr=0; cntr<4; cntr++)
21             {
22             digit = DISTAB[DISPDIGS[cntr]];
23             if (cntr == 0) digit = (digit | 0x01);
24                   /*decimal on if LSD*/
25             for (bitcntr=0; bitcntr<8; bitcntr++)
26                {
27                DDATA = (digit & 0x01);/*output data bit*/
28                CLK = 0;       /*make clock*/
29                CLK = 1;
30                digit = (digit >> 1); /*shift bit*/
31                }
32             }
33          LOAD = 1;   /*load pulse*/
34          LOAD = 0;
35          }
36
37      void convt(unsigned int numbr)
38          {
39          unsigned int temp;
40          unsigned char w;
41          temp = (numbr*25)/64+700; /*calc temperature*/
42          DISPDIGS[3] = temp/1000;/* 1000's digit*/
43          temp = temp % 1000;
44          DISPDIGS[2] = temp/100; /*100's digit*/
45          temp = temp % 100;
46          DISPDIGS[1] = temp/10;   /*10's digit*/
47          temp = temp % 10;
48          DISPDIGS[0] = temp;      /*ones digit*/
49          dispnum();
50          }
51
52      main()
53          {
54          unsigned char q;
```

FIGURE 7–13 Digit conversion module in C.

```
55         unsigned int rawdata;
56         CLK = 1;  /*preset clock*/
57         LOAD = 0; /*preset load*/
58         rawdata = 0x200;  /*90 degrees f*/
59         convt(rawdata);
60         gomon();  /*return to monitor*/
61         }
```

FIGURE 7–13 *continued*

Fahrenheit. This shows the advantage of building modularly on modules known to function correctly.

Using the collection of functional modules, the program for the control buttons may now be written. Figures 7–14 and 7–15 demonstrate the use of the set buttons. The "swcntrl" sections of each program are shown in Figures 7–14 and 7–15. Each of the modules display the set point as soon as the "set" button is depressed and count the set point up or down depending on the button being pressed. The range is checked as the count proceeds up or down to assure that the range of control is not exceeded.

The control loop has been added to the main function and "init" code to begin to show the nature of the final program. A single loop is to be used that will monitor the operation of the device and branch to other functions as required. The program continues to use known good modules while developing new modules.

A delay routine is also added (refer to Chapter 4 for the operation of the delay) to allow the set buttons to repeat if held down. The assembly-language program is changed slightly to use R0 as an indirect pointer to the number to be converted and displayed. In this way either the set point (stored at 32h and 33h) or the sensor data (stored at 30h and 31h) may be displayed.

The next module is to read the A/D with appropriate handshaking. The A/D outputs the high byte as an 8-bit byte and separately outputs the 2 lower bits to make up the 10-bit result. Consequently, the A/D read modules must shift and combine bits into the total result. As shown in Figures 7–16 and 7–17, these two modules simply toggle the convert pin to start the conversion and then wait for a short time to let the conversion finish. The bytes are then read in and shifted as necessary to assemble the entire 10-bit word. The main control loop has been expanded to include a call to the A/D read function so that real data are displayed unless the set switch is pressed. Replacing the sensor with a potentiometer allows testing the system over the entire input range. Arranging the program in this way allows for easy testing of the A/D module.

Finally, the pulse-width output module is created. The module begins with a default value of 50%. In this case the PW drive is based on an interrupt from timer 1. A control number is stored and, as long as the count of passes through the interrupt loop is below the control number, the output is on. For counts above the control number the output is off. Adjusting the control number sets the PW drive to the heater. Figures 7–18 and 7–19 are the modules for the PW control. The programs initialize timer1 to interrupt about every 300 μs. As the count progresses, the output bit is modified according to the relationship of the control number to the loop count. As the control algorithm is developed, it will be used to adjust the output drive.

```
1              ;Switch control module
2         disport equ     0b0h          ;port 3 is display port
3
4              org     2000h
5         start:  ljmp    init          ;jump to init
          NOTE: DISPNUM and CONVT are basically unchanged and
              are deleted form this listing.
93
94        swcntrl:mov     r0,#32h       ;get setpoint data
95             acall   cnvrt         ;display it
96        wtset:  mov     a,disport     ;incr or decr?
97             anl     a,#10h
98             jz      up            ;jump if increment
99             mov     a,disport     ;incr or decr?
100            anl     a,#08h
101            jz      dn            ;jump if decrement
102            mov     a,disport     ;still in set mode?
103            anl     a,#20h
104            jz      wtset         ;jump if yes
105            ret
106       dn:     dec     32h           ;decr LS counter
107            mov     a,32h         ;check for rollover
108            cjne    a,#0ffh,norst
109            dec     33h
110            mov     a,33h         ;check for bottom
111            cjne    a,#0ffh,norst
112            mov     32h,#00       ;reset to lowest
113            mov     33h,#00
114       norst:  mov     r0,#32h       ;display setpoint
115            acall   cnvrt         ;display result
116            mov     b,#1          ;wait 200ms
117            call    delay
118            mov     a,disport     ;incr or decr?
119            anl     a,#20h
120            jz      wtset         ;jump if still set
121            ret
122
123       up:     inc     32h           ;incr LS counter
124            mov     a,32h         ;check for rollover
125            cjne    a,#00h,norst
126            inc     33h
127            mov     a,33h         ;check for top
128            cjne    a,#04h,norst
129            mov     33h,#03h      ;reset top
130            mov     32h,#0ffh
131            sjmp    norst
132
133       delay:  mov     tmod,#21h     ;16 bit count mode
134       delaylp:clr     tr0           ;make sure its off
135            clr     tf0           ;and reset
136            mov     th0,#4ch      ;set for 50ms
137            mov     tl0,#00h
138            setb    tr0           ;start time
139       timlp:  jnb     tf0,timlp     ;wait for time out
```

FIGURE 7–14 Assembly control module.

```
140                 djnz     b,delaylp    ;wait for total time
141                 ret
142
143      init:      clr      disport.2    ;preset load line
144                 setb     disport.1    ;preset clock line
145                 mov      30h,#00h     ;real data from sensor
146                 mov      31h,#02h     ;MS sensor byte
147                 mov      32h,#00h     ;set point LS
148                 mov      33h,#03h     ;set point MS
149      cntrlp:    mov      a,disport    ;check switches
150                 anl      a,#20h       ;mask other stuff
151                 jnz      nosw         ;jump if no switches
152                 acall    swcntrl      ;jump to switch
153      nosw:      mov      r0,#30h      ;point to sensor data
154                 acall    cnvrt        ;display sensor data
155                 ajmp     cntrlp       ;end of active loop
156                 end
```

FIGURE 7–14 *continued*

The control algorithm is the last module to be developed. A variety of control algorithms exist for closed-loop control. These vary from simple on/off control to very complex time-dependent closed-loop controls. In this case the algorithm will be a very simple control based on the error between the set point and the sensor data. Every 0.1 s, the error is checked and the drive incremented or decremented as necessary. The time delay is necessary in order to allow for the slow response of the thermal system. The control modules are shown in Figures 7–20 and 7–21. These two programs work by adding a counter to the interrupt service routine. Each time the counter rolls over, approximately 0.1 s has elapsed. At that time the error between the sensor data and the set point is calculated and the PW control adjusted accordingly. The individual modules and main control loop are now completed.

Test the System Operationally

The project is complete and appears to work correctly. The purpose of the last step is to test the finished project against the specifications. In this project the operational test is conducted using a sensitive temperature-measurement device and running the project for an extended period while recording the results. The incubator is run for 24 h with a measurement taken every 10 min. In this case the result was a maximum variation of 0.6°F from the set point. Unfortunately, this does not meet the ±0.5°F specification. A reasonable approach would be to implement a more stringent control algorithm, but that is beyond the scope of this text.

```
1      #include <reg552.h>
2
3      unsigned char DISPDIGS[4]; /*array to hold digits*/
4      unsigned int sensordata, setpoint;
5      sbit DDATA = 0xb0;   /*data bit*/
6      sbit CLK=0xb1;       /*clock bit*/
7      sbit LOAD=0xb2;      /*load bit*/
8      sbit DOWN=0xb3;      /*down switch*/
9      sbit UP=0xb4;        /*up switch*/
10     sbit SET=0xb5;       /*set switch*/
          NOTE: Dispnum and Convt remain unchanged and
                   are deleted.
53     void delay (unsigned char periods)
54        {
55        TMOD = 0x21;       /*16 bit counter*/
56        while (periods > 0)
57           {
58           TR0 = 0;        /*timer off*/
59           TF0 = 0;        /*clear flag*/
60           TH0 = 0x4c;     /*load for 50ms periods*/
61           TL0 = 0x00;
62           TR0 = 1;        /*start timer*/
63           periods--;      /*decrement periods*/
64           while (TF0 == 0); /*wait timeout*/
65           }
66        }
67
68     void swcntrl(void)
69        {
70        while (SET == 0)
71           {
72           convt(setpoint);   /*display setpoint*/
73           delay(1);   /*wait a bit*/
74           if (UP == 0)
75        {
76        setpoint++;   /*increment setpoint*/
77        if (setpoint > 0x3ff) setpoint = 0x3ff; /*limit*/
78        }
79           if (DOWN == 0)
80        setpoint--;   /*decrement setpoint*/
81        if (setpoint == 0xffff) setpoint=0x0000;/*limit*/
82           }
83        }
84
85     main()
86        {
87        unsigned char q;
88        CLK = 1;   /*preset clock*/
89        LOAD = 0; /*preset load*/
90        sensordata = 0x200;   /*90 degrees f*/
91        setpoint = 0x300; /*100 degrees f*/
92        while (1)
93           {
                                switches*/
95           convt(sensordata);
96           }
97        }
```

FIGURE 7–15 C control module.

```
  1        ;Read A/D module
  2        disport equ    0b0h              ;port 3 is display
  3        adcctrl equ    080h              ;port 0 is adc cntrl
  4        adcdata equ    090h              ;port 1 is adc data
  5
  6                org    2000h
  7        start:  ljmp   init              ;jump to init
         Note: previously shown parts deleted.
145        readad: setb   adcctrl.2         ;start conversion
146                clr    adcctrl.2
147                mov    r6,#20            ;short delay
148        waitad: djnz   r6,waitad
149                clr    adcctrl.1         ;read low byte
150                mov    r0,adcdata        ;read lo data
151                setb   adcctrl.1
152                clr    adcctrl.0         ;read high byte
153                mov    r1,adcdata
154                setb   adcctrl.0
155                mov    a,r0              ;get low byte
156                rl     a                 ;reorder bits
157                rl     a
158                anl    a,#03             ;save valid bits
159                mov    r0,a              ;save bits
160                mov    a,r1              ;get high byte
161                rl     a                 ;reorder bits
162                rl     a
163                push   acc               ;save bits
164                anl    a,#3h             ;get highest byte
165                mov    31h,a             ;save it
166                pop    acc               ;recover bits
167                anl    a,#0fch           ;mask lower byte
168                orl    a,r0              ;or in low bits
169                mov    30h,a             ;save low byte
170                ret
171
172        init:   clr    disport.2         ;preset load line
173                setb   disport.1         ;preset clock line
174                clr    adcctrl.2         ;clear convert line
175                setb   adcctrl.1         ;set low byte enable
176                setb   adcctrl.0         ;set high enable
177                mov    30h,#00h          ;data from sensor
178                mov    31h,#02h          ;MS sensor byte
179                mov    32h,#00h          ;set point LS
180                mov    33h,#03h          ;set point MS
181        cntrlp: mov    a,disport         ;check switches
182                anl    a,#20h            ;mask other stuff
183                jnz    nosw              ;jump if no switches
184                acall  swcntrl           ;jump to switch
185        nosw:   acall  readad            ;get new sensor data
186                mov    r0,#30h           ;sensor data
187                acall  cnvrt             ;display sensor data
188                ajmp   cntrlp            ;end of active loop
189                end
```

FIGURE 7–16 Assembly-language A/D read module.

```
1       #include <reg552.h>
2
3       unsigned char DISPDIGS[4]; /*array to hold digits*/
4       unsigned int sensordata, setpoint;
5       sbit DDATA = 0xb0;   /*data bit*/
6       sbit CLK=0xb1;   /*clock bit*/
7       sbit LOAD=0xb2;   /*load bit*/
8       sbit DOWN=0xb3;   /*down switch*/
9       sbit UP=0xb4;      /*up switch*/
10      sbit SET=0xb5;     /*set switch*/
11      sbit ADCHIGH=0x80; /*read high byte*/
12      sbit ADCLOW=0x81; /*read low byte*/
13      sbit ADCCNVRT=0x82; /*adc convert*/
14      #define ADCDATA P1; /*adc data*/
   Note: previously shown modules deleted
89      unsigned int readad(void)
90         {
91         unsigned char e, lowbyte, highbyte;
92         ADCCNVRT = 1;   /*adc start pulse*/
93         ADCCNVRT = 0;
94         for (e=0; e<20; e++); /*short delay*/
95         ADCLOW = 0;   /*enable low byte*/
96         lowbyte = ADCDATA; /*get low byte*/
97         ADCLOW = 1;
98         ADCHIGH = 0; /*enable high byte*/
99         highbyte = ADCDATA; /*get high byte*/
100        ADCHIGH = 1;
101        return ((highbyte<<2) + ((lowbyte & 0xc0)>>6));
102                 /*combine bytes and return value*/
103        }
104
105     main()
106        {
107        unsigned char q;
108        CLK = 1;   /*preset clock*/
109        LOAD = 0; /*preset load*/
110        ADCCNVRT = 0; /*preset adc convert*/
111        ADCHIGH = 1; /*preset high byte enable*/
112        ADCLOW = 1; /*preset low byte enable*/
113        sensordata = 0x200;   /*90 degrees f*/
114        setpoint = 0x300; /*100 degrees f*/
115        while (1)
116           {
117           swcntrl();   /*check switches*/
118           sensordata = readad();
119           convt(sensordata);
120           }
121        }
```

FIGURE 7–17   C-language A/D read module.

```
  1          ;Display driver module
  2          disport equ     0b0h                    ;port 3 is display
  3          adcctrl equ     080h                    ;port 0 is adc cntrl
  4          adcdata equ     090h                    ;port 1 is adc data
  5
  6                  org     2000h
  7          start:  ljmp    init                    ;jump to init
  8
  9                  org     001bh
 10                  ljmp    pwm                     ;jump to i'rupt
        Note: Previous modules deleted.
172         pwm:    push    acc                     ;save a
173                 inc     35h                     ;bump loop count
174                 mov     a,34h                   ;get control number
175                 clr     c                       ;clear carry
176                 subb    a,35h                   ;subtract loop count
177                 jnc     pwon                    ;turn on pw if high
178                 clr     disport.7               ;turn off PW
179                 pop     acc
180                 reti
181         pwon:   setb    disport.7               ;turn on PW
182                 pop     acc
183                 reti
184
185         init:   clr     disport.2               ;preset load line
186                 setb    disport.1               ;preset clock line
187                 clr     adcctrl.2               ;clear convert line
188                 setb    adcctrl.1               ;low byte enable
189                 setb    adcctrl.0               ;high byte enable
190                 mov     30h,#00h                ;real sensor data
191                 mov     31h,#02h                ;MS sensor byte
192                 mov     32h,#00h                ;set point LS
193                 mov     33h,#03h                ;set point MS
194                 mov     34h,#64                 ;start at 25%
195                 mov     35h,#0                  ;current loop count
196                 mov     TMOD,#21h               ;t1 8-bit autoreload
197                 mov     tl1,#0ffh               ;reload timer
198                 mov     th1,#0ffh
199                 mov     ie,#88h                 ;enable t1 interrupt
200         cntrlp: mov     a,disport               ;check switches
201                 anl     a,#20h                  ;mask other stuff
202                 jnz     nosw                    ;jump if no switches
203                 acall   swcntrl                 ;jump to switch
204         nosw:   acall   readad                  ;get new sensor data
205                 mov     r0,#30h                 ;sensor data
206                 acall   cnvrt                   ;display sensor data
207                 ajmp    cntrlp                  ;end of active loop
208                 end
```

FIGURE 7–18 Assembly-language PW module.

```
1      #include <reg552.h>
2
3      unsigned char DISPDIGS[4], pwcount, pwcntrl;
4      unsigned int sensordata, setpoint;
5      sbit DDATA = 0xb0;   /*data bit*/
6      sbit CLK = 0xb1;   /*clock bit*/
7      sbit LOAD = 0xb2;   /*load bit*/
8      sbit DOWN = 0xb3;   /*down switch*/
9      sbit UP = 0xb4;      /*up switch*/
10     sbit SET = 0xb5;    /*set switch*/
11     sbit PW = 0xb7;     /*PW drive bit*/
12     sbit ADCHIGH = 0x80; /*read high byte*/
13     sbit ADCLOW = 0x81; /*read low byte*/
14     sbit ADCCNVRT = 0x82; /*adc convert*/
15     #define ADCDATA P1; /*adc data*/
       Note previous modules deleted
106    void TM1 (void) interrupt 3 using 2
107        {
108        pwcount++;
109        if (pwcount < pwcntrl) PW = 1;
110        else PW = 0;
111        }
112
113    main()
114        {
115       unsigned char q;
116       CLK = 1;   /*preset clock*/
117       LOAD = 0; /*preset load*/
118       ADCCNVRT = 0; /*preset adc convert*/
119       ADCHIGH = 1; /*preset high byte enable*/
120       ADCLOW = 1; /*preset low byte enable*/
121       pwcntrl = 64; /*25% PW*/
122       TMOD = 0x21; /*t1 set to 8 bit reload*
123       TL1 = 0xff; /*reload number*/
124       TH1 = 0xff;
125       IE = 0x88; /*enable t1 interrupt*/
126       setpoint = 0x300; /*100 degrees f*/
127       while (1)
128           {
129           swcntrl();   /*check switches*/
130           sensordata = readad();
131           convt(sensordata);
132           }
133        }
```

FIGURE 7–19   C-language PW module.

```
  1        ;Control module
  2        disport equ     0c0h              ;port 3 is display
  3        adcctrl equ     080h              ;port 0 is adc cntrl
  4        adcdata equ     090h              ;port 1 is adc data
  5
  6                org     2000h
  7        start:  ljmp    init              ;jump to init
           Note: Previous modules deleted
172        pwm:    push    acc               ;save registers
173                push    PSW
174                inc     36h               ;incr cntrl loop cnt
175                mov     a,36h             ;get cntrl loop cnt
176                cjne    a,#00,nlp         ;jmp if no cntrl adj
177                clr     c                 ;set for subtraction
178                mov     a,31h             ;get high byte
179                subb    a,33h             ;subtract high set
180                jc      toohigh           ;reduce drive
181                jnz     toolow            ;increase drive
182                clr     c                 ;must be equal
183                mov     a,30h             ;get low sensor byte
184                subb    a,32h             ;check difference
185                jc      toohigh           ;reduce drive
186                jnz     toolow            ;increase drive
187                sjmp    nlp               ;no change
188        toohigh:dec     34h               ;reduce pwcntrl
189                mov     a,34h             ;check limit
190                cjne    a,#0ffh,nlp       ;check for minimum
191                mov     34h,#0
192                sjmp    nlp
193        toolow: inc     34h               ;increase pwcntrl
194                mov     a,34h             ;check limit
195                cjne    a,#00h,nlp        ;check for maximum
196                mov     34h,#0ffh
197        nlp:    inc     35h               ;bump loop count
198                mov     a,34h             ;get control number
199                clr     c                 ;clear carry
200                subb    a,35h             ;subtract loop count
201                jnc     pwon              ;turn on pw if high
202                clr     disport.7         ;turn off PW
203                pop     PSW
204                pop     acc
205                reti
206        pwon:   setb    disport.7         ;turn on PW
207                pop     PSW
208                pop     acc
209                reti
```

FIGURE 7–20 Assembly-language control module.

```
               Note Previous modules deleted
106               void TM1 (void) interrupt 3 using 2
107                 {
108    1            pwcount++;
109    1            if (pwcount < pwcntrl) PW = 1;
110    1            else PW = 0;
111    1            adjcnt++;   /*bump adjust counter*/
112    1            if (adjcnt == 0)
113    1              {
114    2                if (sensordata > setpoint)
115    2            {
116    3          pwcntrl--;   /* reduce heat*/
117    3          if (pwcntrl == 0xff) pwcntrl = 0; /*limit*/
118    3            }
119    2                if (sensordata < setpoint)
120    2            {
121    3          pwcntrl++;   /*increase heat*/
122    3          if (pwcntrl == 0x00) pwcntrl=0xff;/*limit*/
123    3            }
124    2              }
125    1            }
```

FIGURE 7–21   C-language control module.

7–6   A KEYLESS ENTRY SYSTEM

A keyless entry system is composed of two computers, one at the door as a remote to identify those wishing to enter or exit, and one, usually a PC, to keep records and authorize entry. The computers communicate via a serial data link. The final implementation could carry the signal by wire, infrared, or radio signal, depending on the application. This project will use a wire medium for simplicity.

Define the Scope of the Project

This project implements an expandable basic access security system. The project is to design the microcontroller remote end of an ''airlock'' access system.

The basic scheme is that when the system recognizes a person who wants to go in or out, it checks with the main computer to determine if the person should be allowed access. For example, people trying to enter the building would identify themselves, and the remote computer would communicate the request to the main computer. Assuming that the main computer finds they are authorized to enter, it sends a command to the remote that begins the access sequence. First it unlocks the outer door. After the people pass inside and the outer door is closed, the controller relocks it and unlocks the inner door to allowing the people to enter the premises. The reverse occurs when someone wishes to exit the building. Only one door is unlocked at any time, limiting access. A major advantage of such a system is that the main computer can keep records of the times at which people come and go. Further, the system can restrict access to any person at certain hours.

The major weakness of most such systems is that they rely on a key or badge reader to activate or deactivate the system. Anyone with minimum electronic skill can read and reproduce the key. This system will circumvent the problem by using an electronic identity device that contains a reprogrammable code. The system will change the code randomly each time the lock is activated by the device.

The project is to develop the remote microcontroller for such a system. The microcontroller is responsible for reading the identity device, communicating with the main PC serially, and controlling the access sequence for the doors.

The specifications for the remote microcontroller access system are:

Communicates serially with the PC

Uses an electronic ''key''

Controls the ''airlock'' doors

Provides for future expansion and sophistication

Given the specifications, a basic block diagram may be constructed. The block diagram in Figure 7–22 shows the extent of the required devices, but assumes nothing about their nature.

Design/Plan the Hardware and Software

Designing the hardware for this project will follow the easiest path. Those blocks that are most easily designed will be done first. Likewise, the simplest possible hardware for the door will be assumed.

FIGURE 7–22 Access system block diagram.

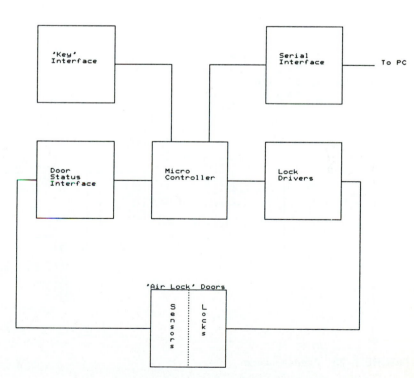

The door sensors are to allow the microcontroller to tell whether the doors are open or closed. This design uses microswitches on the doors, which are normally open and which close when the door is closed. No interface will be required other than a pull-up resistor.

The electronic locks used on doors are usually solenoid devices requiring high-power voltage control to operate. A power MOSFET driver similar to the one in Figure 7–7 may be used to drive these devices. Additional components are added to protect the MOSFET from inductive "spikes."

The serial interface chosen is a MAXIM MAX233 as applied in Chapter 4.

The challenge in this project is the programmable key device. In this case a Dallas Semiconductor DS1991 is selected based on the fact that it meets the programmability requirement and it is durable and not damaged by handling. The device has features well beyond those applied in this project, which allows for later system enhancement.

The DS1991 is a two-terminal device that can communicate with a microcontroller using the terminals as a bidirectional serial bus. One of the terminals is ground and the other is the serial bus. The application information for the device shows that only a pull-up resistor is required to interface the device to a microcontroller.

Review of the paragraphs above show that 2 output bits are required to control the door locks, 2 input bits are required to sense the door status, 1 I/O bit is required to interface to the identity key, and 2 bits are required for serial communication with the PC. The project requires 5 bits of I/O plus serial communication. These requirements are best met by use of an 87C51 microcontroller. The complete tentative schematic is given in Figure 7–23.

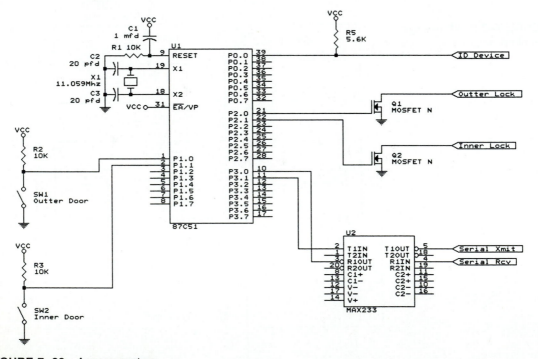

FIGURE 7–23 Access system.

The final steps to this phase of the project are the software development plan and planning the development hardware. Review of the documentation with the DS1991 reveals very tight timing requirements for communication. This suggests that assembly language would be a good choice for the project. The balance of the project is relatively simple, and so the effort necessary to combine assembly and C-language modules is unwarranted.

The development system will be an SBC based on an 80C552.

Build and Test the Hardware

Developing the hardware again follows the path in which the parts of the project contribute to the ability to test other parts. The serial port is developed first, followed by the door controls/sensors. The pull-up for the ID device does not really require testing.

The MAX233 integrated circuit may be built up and then tested using the PC. After construction, connect the output from the MAX233 (pin 3) to its input (pin 2). Using a terminal emulator on the PC, type some test characters. They are transmitted by the PC serially, then looped back to the PC's serial input through the MAX233. They should appear on the screen, showing that the MAX233 is functional.

The door controls and sensors are conveniently tested as a group. Build up the circuits, then connect one switch input to one lock driver gate (i.e., pin 1 on the 87C51 to pin 21 on the 87C51). Toggling the switch should cause the lock to engage and disengage. The other set of controls can be tested similarly.

Write and Test the Software

There are three distinct modules for this project: The first is the serial communications module to send and receive messages, the second is the access sequence to control the doors, and the third is to read and write the identity device.

The serial communications functions are the same as presented previously, plus one new function to send or receive a series of 6 bytes to/from the host PC. This module is used to send/receive the identification data. Figure 7–24 shows the serial communications functions and test code. The program uses the serial and delay routines from Chapter 4. It adds two routines to transmit and receive 6 bytes using the serial port. These routines pass a value in r0 for the routines to use as an indirect pointer to the storage area for the bytes to be either sent or received. The "6 byte" routines are needed for the identity device.

The "init" module initializes the serial port and timers to allow the serial communications and time-delay routines to function. This module then waits for a byte to be received serially. If the byte is an ASCII 0, the program jumps to test the "get6" and "send6" routines. Otherwise it adds 1 to the byte and returns it. This allows testing the serial send and receive routines first, then when they are known to be working, pressing 0 allows the test of the get6 and send6 routines. The get6 and send6 routines simply get the next six characters typed and return them when all six have been typed.

The door-access sequence module is tested next. This module unlocks the outer door, waits for it to open and close, then relocks the outer door and repeats the sequence for the inner door. The outer door and inner door modules are written as separate modules,

```
1           ;Security Access System
2
3                   org      2000h
4           start:  ljmp     init              ;jump to init
5
6           ;transmits byte in a
7           serout: jnb      ti,serout         ;ready?
8                   clr      ti                ;clear for next time
9                   mov      sbuf,a            ;send byte
10                  ret
11
12          ;returns received byte in a
13          serin:  clr      ri                ;clear for next time
14                  mov      a,sbuf            ;get byte
15                  ret
16
17          ;sends 6 bytes - first byte address in r0
18          send6:  mov      r1,#6             ;six bytes
19          sen6lp: mov      a,@r0             ;get byte
20                  inc      r0                ;bump pointer
21                  acall    serout            ;send it
22                  djnz     r1,sen6lp         ;repeat as required
23                  ret
24
25          ;receives 6 bytes places them starting at addr in r0
26          get6:   mov      r1,#6             ;six bytes
27          get6lp: jnb      ri,get6lp         ;wait for character
28                  acall    serin             ;get byte
29                  mov      @r0,a             ;store it
30                  inc      r0                ;bump pointer
31                  djnz     r1,get6lp         ;repeat until 6
32                  ret
33
34          ;waits 50ms*b
35          delay:  clr      tf0               ;t0 overflow reset
36                  mov      th0,#4ch          ;delay time
37                  mov      tl0,#00
38                  setb     tr0               ;t0 on
39          timlop: jnb      tf0,timlop        ;wait 50 ms
40                  clr      tr0               ;t0 off
41                  djnz     b,delay
42                  ret
43
44          init:   mov      scon,#052h        ;8 bin UART
45                  mov      tmod,#021h        ;Set timer modes!
46                  mov      tcon,#0           ;nothing running
47                  mov      th1,#0fdh         ;9600 baud
48                  setb     tr1               ;start serial
49
50          notyet: jnb      ri,notyet         ;wait for char.
51                  acall    serin             ;get character
52                  cjne     a,#30h,notzero    ;zero?
53                  sjmp     sixtest           ;jump if zero
54          notzero:inc      a                 ;incr character
```

FIGURE 7–24 Serial communications module.

```
55                acall    serout         ;return it
56                sjmp     notyet         ;again and again
57     sixtest:mov         r0,#30h        ;set storage area
58                acall    get6           ;get 6 characters
59                mov      r0,#30h        ;point to string
60                acall    send6          ;send 6 characters
61                sjmp     notyet         ;repeat
62                end
```

FIGURE 7–24   *continued*

which are called by one of two subroutines depending on the direction of the sequence (in or out of the secured area).

Figure 7–25 shows the test software for the ''airlock'' doors. The ''goin'' and ''goout'' routines call the ''inseq'' and ''outseq'' routines in opposite order to accomplish the airlock control. Each employs a time delay to allow for switch bounce in the door sensor and a second check on the status of the door to assure that the sequence is completed correctly. The serial routines are used to simulate the commands from the PC. An ASCII 0 will activate the goout sequence, and any other character will activate the goin sequence.

The final module to be developed is the ID device interface software. The module must read the device's ID code and the data written to the device during the previous entry. The ID code and data are reported to the PC serially. The PC then responds with new data to be written into the ID device. The new data are used next time the device is used to secure access.

The ID device works by responding to the microcontroller's commands as a slave to the microcontroller. The only signal initiated by the ID device is the presence pulse. The device has an internal battery and holds the two terminals of the device at the same potential while not connected to a circuit. This is the reset condition for the device.

When attached to the microcontroller, the pull-up resistor pulls the signal line of the ID device high with respect to the ground, awakening the ID device. The ID device issues a 60-μs low pulse on the signal line, which is sensed by the microcontroller to detect the presence of the ID device.

In order to communicate with the device, the microcontroller must first recognize the device as present. Next the microcontroller holds the ID line low for a period to cause an additional reset. When the ID line is released returning to a logic high, the ID device again responds with a presence pulse, which is sensed by the microcontroller. This reset/ response sequence establishes that the signals on the ID line are from the ID device and not from noise.

Following the sequence to assure that the ID device is real, the microcontroller issues a command word. The first command word is 0x33, the command to read the device ID. The process of writing (either command or data) to the device involves serially sending 1 bit at a time using the ID line. Each bit is preceded by a 1 μs (or longer) low-going pulse followed by the bit level held for at least 60 μs. The ID line must then be returned high (if it was not outputting a high bit) to make the 1-μs pulse for the next bit.

The 0x33 command word causes the ID device to respond with its 8-byte identification code. The process of reading the ID device is similar to writing to it. The microcon-

```
 1          ;Sercurity Access System
 2    outdr    equ      P1.0                  ;outter door sense
 3    indr     equ      P1.1                  ;inner door sense
 4    outlk    equ      P2.0                  ;outter lock
 5    inlk     equ      P2.1                  ;inner lock
 6    id       equ      P0.0                  ;id device
      Note: Previously discussed sections deleted
49    outseq: clr      outlk                 ;unlock outter door
50    waitout:jnb      outdr,waitout         ;wait for door open
51            mov      b,#5                  ;wait-sw bounce
52            acall    delay
53            jnb      outdr,waitout         ;doublecheck
54    waito2: jb       outdr,waito2          ;wait while open
55            mov      b,#5                  ;wait for sw bounce
56            acall    delay
57            jb       outdr,waito2          ;doublecheck
58            setb     outlk                 ;relock door
59            ret
60
61    inseq:  clr      inlk                  ;unlock inner door
62    waitin: jnb      indr,waitin           ;wait for door open
63            mov      b,#5                  ;wait-sw bounce
64            acall    delay
65            jnb      indr,waitin           ;doublecheck
66    waiti2: jb       indr,waiti2           ;wait while open
67            mov      b,#5                  ;wait for sw bounce
68            acall    delay
69            jb       indr,waiti2           ;doublecheck
70            setb     inlk                  ;relock door
71            ret
72
73    goout:  acall    inseq                 ;open inner door
74            acall    outseq                ;open outter door
75            ret
76
77    goin:   acall    outseq                ;open outter door
78            acall    inseq
79            ret
80
81    init:   mov      scon,#052h            ;8 bin UART
82            mov      tmod,#021h            ;Set timer modes!
83            mov      tcon,#0               ;nothing running
84            mov      th1,#0fdh             ;9600 baud
85            setb     tr1                   ;start serial
86
87    notyet: jnb      ri,notyet             ;wait for char.
88            acall    serin                 ;get character
89            cjne     a,#30h,notzero        ;zero?
90            acall    goout                 ;jump if zero
91            sjmp     notyet                ;repeat
92    notzero:acall    goin                  ;incr character
93            sjmp     notyet                ;repeat
94            end
```

FIGURE 7–25   Airlock sequence module.

troller again makes the 1-μs pulse. The ID device then holds the data for the bit in either a high or a low for 15 μs. During this period the microcontroller must read the bit value. Following the read the microcontroller must waste the rest of the 60-μs bit period before issuing the next pulse.

Similar sequences are followed to issue the command to read the scratch area and to receive the data from the scratch area (the random code data written during the previous entry). The received code and data are reported to the PC and new data are received to be written into the ID device. Again the reset/response sequence and the ID are read from the device. Then, the command to write data is issued, and new data are written to the scratch area. Finally, a code is received from the PC to start either the goin or the goout access sequence.

Figure 7–26 shows the functions to read and write the ID device. The important feature of these functions is their timing. Looking at "rbyte," lines 95 and 96 make the 1-μs (or slightly longer) pulse. The important timing takes place in lines 97 through 98. The timing is shown as follows:

```
27              mov   r2,#3        takes 12 clock periods
28   holdr:  djnz  r2,holdr    takes 24 × 3 = 72 clock periods
          84 clock periods × 1/11.0592 Mhz = 7.6 μs
```

This loop consumes 7.6 μs to allow time for the ID device to output the first data bit. Lines 99 and 100 read the bit by moving it to the carry and then rotating it into the MSB of the accumulator. They also consume another 24 clock periods. The loop in lines 101 and 102 and in line 103 uses a total of 612 clock periods. Together these steps use 55.3 μs before looping back to read the next bit. Altogether these steps use 62.9 μs as compared to the minimum specification of 60 μs. This is also an example of the method used to provide a critically timed routine. The "wrbyte" routine works similarly, except that the data remain on the pin for 60 μs to allow time for the ID device to read it.

Figure 7–27 shows the main program loop. Line 136 waits for the presence pulse on the ID line. When a pulse is detected, the program sends the commands and reads data as described above to allow a person to enter or leave through the airlock.

This system works as designed, but has certain drawbacks. The first is that there is only one ID sensor connection, making it difficult to have a sensor inside for those who want out and outside for those who want in. Fortunately, the ID device is a bus device, and a connector for the device may be placed both outside and inside. As long as both are not used simultaneously, the system will function. The PC will need to remember which IDs are inside and which are currently outside so that the correct door sequence is used. Similarly, the system does not allow for various exceptions such as when the door is opened and closed before anyone goes through. The program at the PC could be designed to handle some of these.

Test the System Operationally

Finally, the system is run using the doors, locks, and PC to complete a final test.

```
1            ;Security Access System
2    outdr   equ      P1.0          ;outter door sense
3    indr    equ      P1.1          ;inner door sense
4    outlk   equ      P2.0          ;outter lock
5    inlk    equ      P2.1          ;inner lock
6    id      equ      P0.0          ;id device
7
     Note: previously discussed modules deleted
94   rbyte:  mov      r3,#8         ;read 8 bits
95   rblp:   clr      id            ;make pulse
96           setb     id
97           mov      r2,#3         ;waste 8 usecs
98   holdr:  djnz     r2,holdr
99           mov      c,id          ;get data bit
100          rrc      a             ;move into a
101          mov      r2,#24        ;waste 55 usecs
102  holdr2: djnz     r2,holdr2
103          djnz     r3,rblp       ;done 8 bits yet?
104          ret
105
106  wrbyte: mov      r3,#8         ;write 8 bits
107  wrblp:  clr      id            ;make pulse
108          rrc      a             ;move data bit to c
109          mov      id,c          ;move C to data pin
110          mov      r2,#26        ;waste 60 usecs
111  holdw:  djnz     r2,holdw
112          setb     id            ;finish sync pulse
113          djnz     r3,wrblp      ;done 8 bits yet?
114          ret
115
116  read8:  mov      r1,#8         ;get 8 bytes
117  rd8lp:  acall    rbyte         ;get byte from id
118          mov      @r0,a         ;store byte
119          inc      r0            ;bump pointer
120          djnz     r1,rd8lp      ;8 bytes yet?
121          ret
122
123  write8: mov      r1,#8         ;write 8 bytes
124  wr8lp:  mov      a,@r0         ;get data byte
125          acall    wrbyte        ;write byte to id
126          inc      r0            ;bump data pointer
127          djnz     r1,wr8lp      ;8 bytes yet?
128          ret
129
130  init:   mov      scon,#052h    ;8 bin UART
131          mov      tmod,#021h    ;Set timer modes!
132          mov      tcon,#0       ;nothing running
133          mov      th1,#0fdh     ;9600 baud
134          setb     tr1           ;start serial
```

FIGURE 7–26   ID device module functions.

```
136    main:    jb      id,main         ;wait for code
137             clr     id              ;force reset
138             mov     b,#1            ;short delay
139             acall   delay
140             setb    id              ;finish reset
141    main2:   jb      id,main2
142    waitst:  jnb     id,waitst       ;wait end of pulse
143             mov     a,#33h          ;read id command
144             acall   wrbyte          ;send command to id
145             mov     r0,#20h         ;point to id array
146             acall   read8           ;get 8 byte id
147             mov     a,#69h          ;read scratch cmnd
148             acall   wrbyte          ;send it
149             mov     a,#0c0h         ;second cmnd byte
150             acall   wrbyte          ;send it
151             mov     a,#3fh          ;third command byte
152             acall   wrbyte          ;send it
153             mov     r0,#28h         ;store code data
154             acall   read8           ;get 8 data bytes
155             mov     r0,#20h         ;point to id
156             acall   send8           ;send to pc
157             mov     r0,#28h         ;point to data
158             acall   send8           ;send to pc
159             mov     r0,#28h         ;point to data
160             acall   get8            ;get new data
161             clr     id              ;force reset
162             mov     b,#1            ;short delay
163             acall   delay
164             setb    id              ;finish reset
165    main3:   jb      id,main3
166    waitss:  jnb     id,waitss       ;wait end of pulse
167             mov     a,#33h          ;read id command
168             acall   wrbyte          ;send command to id
169             mov     r0,#20h         ;point to id array
170             acall   read8           ;get 8 byte id
171
172             mov     a,#96h          ;write scratch cmnd
173             acall   wrbyte          ;send it
174             mov     a,#0c0h         ;second cmnd byte
175             acall   wrbyte          ;send it
176             mov     a,#3fh          ;third command byte
177             acall   wrbyte          ;send it
178             mov     r0,#28h         ;point to new data
179             acall   write8          ;xfer new id data
180    waitcmd: jnb     ri,waitcmd      ;get in or out cmnd
181             acall   serin           ;get command
182             cjne    a,#0fh,notin    ;check for in
183             acall   goin            ;do in sequence
184             sjmp    main            ;all done
185    notin:   acall   goout           ;do out sequence
186             sjmp    main            ;all done
```

FIGURE 7–27   ID main loop.

7-7   REMOTE DATA COLLECTION SYSTEM

Many situations require the collection of data over intervals covering an extended period of time. Examples are environmental conditions at remote sites, environmental conditions in an office or home, conditions relative to automobile engine operation, or other situations in which samples over a long interval are required. People seldom remember to measure faithfully, but microcontrollers are outstanding at this sort of job.

Define the Scope of the Project

This project is to develop a multipurpose system to gather analog data over a period of time. The system may be adapted to a variety of recording tasks by the addition of suitable analog interfaces.

At least four analog channels are to be recorded at intervals of 1 min up to 1 h. The analog data is to be recorded with a minimum resolution of 8 bits. The data and system control are to be via RS232 serial communication with a PC. Specifications for the remote data collection system are:

> Data recording of four analog channels at 0–5 VDC
>
> Data accuracy to 8 bits resolution
>
> Serial control of sampling interval and data transfer
>
> Sampling intervals of 1 min to 1 h in 1-min steps
>
> Minimum recording ability of 1000 data points
>
> Data must be retained even if power fails
>
> Battery operation (minimum power consumption)

These specifications suggest the block diagram shown in Figure 7–28. The block diagram shows a microcontroller with serial interface, A/D conversion, and memory for data storage. Up to now the memory has not been shown specifically as a part of the block diagram. It is shown in this instance due to the need for significant memory as part of the project.

FIGURE 7–28 Data collection system block diagram.

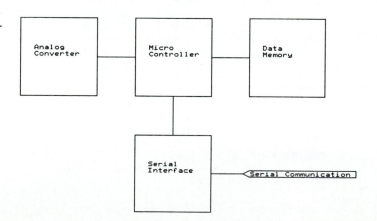

Design/Plan the Hardware and Software

The serial interface has been discussed in the previous project and is included in this project without further discussion.

The A/D converter needs to be a multichannel device capable of 0–5 VDC measurement and a resolution of 8 bits.

The memory section requires either nonvolatile storage or battery backup for data retention. In this case absolute protection is offered only by nonvolatile memory. EEPROM is chosen as a nonvolatile form of storage requiring no external circuitry or special voltages to function.

This project is an opportunity to apply the 80C552 microcontroller. This device is made by Signetics and features the 8051 core plus an 8-channel, 10-bit A/D converter, an extended timer array, two PWM channels, and additional parallel I/O ports. In this instance the device provides the A/D converter as well as the timing and controller functions. The only additions needed are the serial interface, program memory, and the EEPROM data memory. A tentative schematic is shown in Figure 7–29. It is a standard implementation of bus-connected microcontroller components.

Build and Test the Hardware

The serial section of this project is developed and tested as discussed previously and will not be reiterated here.

The A/D section is developed next. The A/D converter on the 80C552 is controlled, as are all of the internal peripherals, via a set of SFRs. In this case the SFRs are ADCON and ADCH. ADCON contains the control and status bits for the ADC as well as the lower 2 bits of the 10-bit conversion result. ADCH contains the upper 8 bits of the conversion result.

Figure 7–30 shows the bits that make up the ADC SFRs. The ADC is controlled by setting the address of the channel to measure into bits 0, 1, and 2. The ADCS bit is then set high to start the conversion. ADCS is held high during the conversion as an indicator that the ADC is busy. Upon completion of a conversion, ADCI is set high and will cause an interrupt if the A/D interrupt is enabled. When complete, the most significant 8 bits of the result reside in ADCH. The ADC is not separate hardware and so must be tested by software.

Figures 7–31 and 7–32 are programs to read channel 0 repeatedly and to send the result as two ASCII digits (1 hex byte) to a serial terminal. The program in Figure 7–31 shows the test program to read channel 0 of the built-in A/D and to output the result as a byte displayed on a serial terminal. Lines 57 and 58 set the channel to be read (in this case 0) and then call the ''adread'' routine. The operation of the A/D may be discovered by studying this routine. Basically, ADCON is loaded with the channel number in the least significant bits, then the start bit is set high (line 43 ORs the start bit in with the channel number), and finally the program waits for ADCI to go high, indicating completion. The value read is returned to the main program for display. Note that the serial display routines are from Chapter 4.

Figure 7–32 is the C-language program to accomplish the same task. Its operation is identical to the assembly-language program.

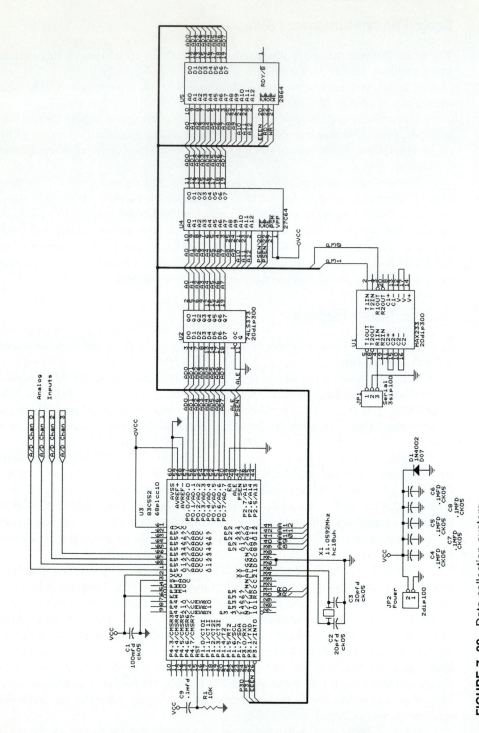

FIGURE 7–29 Data collection system.

148

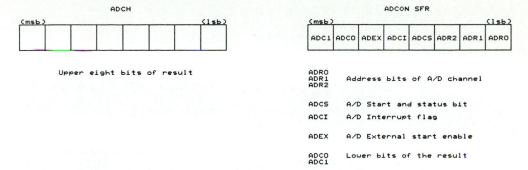

FIGURE 7-30   ADCON register.

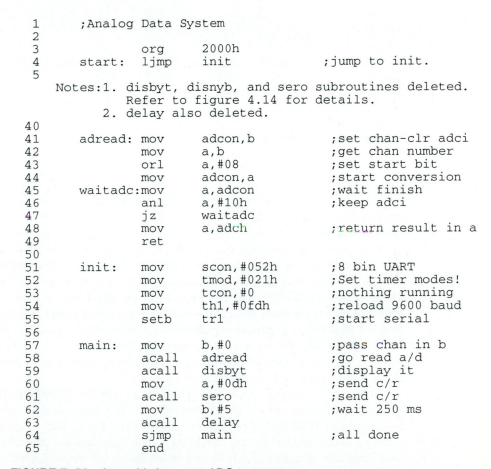

FIGURE 7-31   Assembly-language ADC test program.

```
1      /*Analog Data System*/
2      #include <absacc.h>
3      #include <reg552.h>
4
       Note:   Serial and display routines deleted
59
60     unsigned char adread (unsigned char channel)
61        {
62        ADCON = channel;    /*set channel & clear ADCI*/
63        ADCON = (channel | 0x8);  /*start conversion*/
64        while ((ADCON & 0x10) == 0); /*wait finish*/
65        return ADCH;    /*return converted value*/
66        }
67
68
69     void main (void)
70        {
71        S0CON = 0x52;     /*8 bit uart*/
72        TMOD = 0x21;      /*timer modes*/
73        TH1 = 0xfd;       /*9600 baud*/
74        TR1 = 1;          /*start timer*/
75
76        for (;;)
77           {
78           disbyt(adread(0)); /*read & disp chan 0*/
79           sero(0x0d);    /*CR*/
80           delay(5);   /*delay 1/2 second*/
81           }
82        }
```

FIGURE 7–32   C-language ADC test program.

The data storage portion of the program may be developed next. Conceptually, the external data storage may be treated as an external array consisting of 8196 cells. Each cell holds one reading by the A/D. Testing the data storage amounts to filling the array, removing power, and checking the contents of the array when power is restored.

The external data RAM consists of EEPROM. Writing to EEPROM in this application amounts to writing the data and then assuring that the write cycle is complete before attempting to write further data. This project records only 1 byte at a time, meaning that allowance need not be made for multiple-page writes and other complications. The program allows at least 100 μs to pass, then monitors the location that was written until the correct data are found. The 100 μs is the delay period between the last write and the automatic start of a write cycle. During the write cycle the memory outputs all 0s except the MSB, which is the complement of the data being written.

Figures 7–33 and 7–34 are test programs to test the EEPROM. The assembly-language test program uses a loop in lines 67–72. The data pointer is used to point to the current EEPROM storage cell and the data are passed in A. The "wreepr" subroutine writes the data, waits 100 μs, and checks the cell until the data matches what was written. The C-language program uses a FOR loop to call the wreepr function, which accomplishes the write. Note that the assembly-language program writes 0xff down to 0x00 in successive

```
 1          ;Analog Data System
 2          dataloc data    3000h      ;data storage
       Note: Previously discussed sections deleted.
52          wreepr: movx    @dptr,a           ;write to EEPROM
53                  mov     r1,a              ;save data
54                  mov     r0,#47            ;100 microsec delay
55          wrdlp:  djnz    r0,wrdlp
56          wrlop:  movx    a,@dptr           ;get current data
57                  cjne    a,01,wrlop        ;01 = r1
58                  ret
59
60
61          init:   mov     scon,#052h        ;8 bin UART
62                  mov     tmod,#021h        ;Set timer modes!
63                  mov     tcon,#0           ;nothing running
64                  mov     th1,#0fdh         ;reload value
65                  setb    tr1               ;start serial
66
67          main:   mov     dptr,#dataloc     ;poin to array
68                  mov     r2,#0ffh          ;try 255 locations
69          mnlop:  mov     a,r2              ;test data
70                  acall   wreepr            ;go write it
71                  inc     dptr              ;bump pointer
72                  djnz    r2,mnlop          ;done yet?
73
74                  ljmp    0030h             ;return to monitor
75                  end
```

FIGURE 7–33 Assembly-language EEPROM test program.

```
 1      /*Analog Data System*/
 2      #include <absacc.h>
 3      #include <reg552.h>
 4      xdata unsigned char adata[8196];
 5      unsigned char x;
     Note:  Previously discussed sections deleted.
70      void wreepr (unsigned int where, unsigned char what)
71          {
72          unsigned char tim;
73          adata[where]= what;      /*write data*/
74          for (tim=0;tim<40;tim++);  /*short delay*/
75          while(adata[where] != what);/*wait write cycle*/
76          }
77
78      void main (void)
79          {
80          S0CON = 0x52;      /*8 bit uart*/
81          TMOD = 0x21;       /*timer modes*/
82          TH1 = 0xfd;        /*9600 baud*/
83          TR1 = 1;           /*start timer*/
84          for (x=0;x<0xff;x++)wreepr(x,x);
85
86          gomon();           /*return to monitor*/
87          }
```

FIGURE 7–34 C-language EEPROM test program.

```
 1        ;Analog Data System
 2              org     0100h              ;set above i'rupts
      Note: Previously discussed code deleted.
61        readall:mov     r3,#00h            ;clear channel cntr
62        rdall:  mov     b,r3               ;pass channel in b
63                acall   adread             ;get data
64                acall   wreepr             ;put into EEPROM
65                inc     dptr               ;bump data pointer
66                inc     r3                 ;bump counter
67                cjne    r3,#4,rdall        ;not done yet?
68                ret
69
70        init:   mov     scon,#052h         ;8 bin UART
71                mov     tmod,#021h         ;Set timer modes
72                mov     tcon,#0            ;nothing running
73                mov     th1,#0fdh          ;reload for 9600
74                setb    tr1                ;start serial
75
76        main:   jnb     ri,main            ;wait for char.
77                clr     ri                 ;clear rcv flag
78                mov     a,sbuf             ;get byte
79                mov     r7,a               ;save byte
80                clr     c                  ;clear c for subb
81                subb    a,#60              ;greater than 60?
82                jnc     xfer               ;jump to transfer
83        record: mov     r5,#20             ;preload msecs cntr
84                mov     r4,#60             ;preload secs cntr
85                mov     dptr,#dataloc      ;point to data
86                acall   readall            ;first data set
87                mov     a,r7               ;get #minutes
88                mov     r6,a               ;save in r6
89                mov     th0,#4ch           ;delay time 50ms
90                mov     tl0,#00
91                setb    tr0                ;t0 on
92                mov     ie,#082h           ;enable interrupt
93        idle:   orl     pcon,#01           ;invoke idle mode
94                sjmp    idle               ;return to idle
95        xfer:   mov     dptr,#dataloc      ;point to data
96                mov     r3,#8              ;digit counter
97        inxfrlp:mov     r6,0ffh            ;digit counter
98        xfrlp:  mov     r5,#4              ;data sets counter
99        setlp:  movx    a,@dptr            ;get data
100               inc     dptr               ;bump pointer
101               acall   sero               ;xfer data
102               cjne    r5,#1,comma        ;check for 4th byte
103               sjmp    nocomma            ;don't xfer comma
104       comma:  mov     a,#','             ;xfer comma
105               acall   ser2               ;xfer it
106       nocomma:djnz    r5,setlp           ;send 4 bytes
107               mov     a,#0dh             ;xfer CR
108               acall   ser2               ;xfer it
109               djnz    r6,xfrlp           ;inner loop counter
110               djnz    r3,inxfrlp         ;outter loop cntr
```

FIGURE 7–35 Assembly-language data collection system.

```
111                     ljmp     init                     ;reset
112
114                     org      000bh                    ;t0 interrupt
115        t0isrv: mov          th0,#4ch                 ;reload timer
116                     mov      tl0,#00
117                     djnz     r5,idun                  ;1 second up?
118                     mov      r5,#20                   ;reload
119                     djnz     r4,idun                  ;1 minute up?
120                     mov      r4,#60                   ;reload secs
121                     djnz     r6,idun                  ;record yet?
122                     mov      06,r7                    ;reload #mins
124                     lcall    readall                  ;get data
125        idun:   reti
126
127                     end
```

FIGURE 7–35   *continued*

cells, while the C-language program writes 0x00 up to 0xff in successive cells. This is to allow adequate testing. The nonvolatile nature of EEPROM means that the results of the previous test are still in the memory, and successive tests must alter the cells to assure that the program is actually writing to the EEPROM.

This concludes the hardware testing portion of the data collection system.

Write and Test the Software

Two sections of the software remain to be written, along with the main program loop. These are the formatted output routine and the timing routine. The timing routine is developed first.

The project requirements set forth a time period of 1 min to 60 min. Ideally, the project would go into idle mode for the entire time period to conserve power, then wake up and record one 4-byte set of data samples. Unfortunately, the timers are not capable of such extended periods without processor intervention. The longest time period the timers can handle is 65,536 clock periods (approximately 71 ms). As this is an inconvenient number to work with, the next lowest convenient number is used: 50 ms. This 50-ms time-out causes an interrupt, and the interrupt service routine controls the recording of data.

The program is written so that upon power-up, the data collector waits for a single serial byte. This byte is the number of minutes between each sample. When this character is received, the data collection starts and continues until the device is turned off.

The formatted data transfer routine also makes use of the serial byte at power-up. If the byte is greater than 60 (the maximum number of minutes per sample), then the program enters the routine to transfer the formatted data to a serial host. The format of the data is comma-delimited data. That is, each set of 4 bytes is separated by commas, and the sets are separated by a carriage return and line feed. Many spreadsheet programs can make use of data in this format.

The main program, then, simply waits for the serial byte either to set up the time for sampling or to transfer the data. If the transfer command is received, the data are sent

```
  1    /*Analog Data System*/
       Note: Previously discussed parts deleted.
 79    void TM0() interrupt 1 using 2
 80       {
 81       unsigned char w;
 82       TH0 = 0x4c;  /*load for 50ms periods*/
 83       TL0 = 0x00;
 84       if (timecount++ == timereload)
 85          {
 86          timecount = 0; /*reset interval*/
 87          for (w=0; w<4; w++) wreepr(x++,adread(w));
 88                          /*read analog data*/
 89          }
 90       }
 91
 92    void main (void)
 93       {
 94       SCON = 0x52;     /*8 bit uart*/
 95       TMOD = 0x21;     /*timer modes*/
 96       TH1 = 0xfd;      /*9600 baud*/
 97       TR1 = 1;         /*start timer*/
 98       x=0;
 99       while (RI == 0); /*wait for character*/
100       if (SBUF <= 60) /*Check character*/
101          {
102          for (w=0; w<4; w++) wreepr(x++,adread(w));
103          TH0 = 0x4c;  /*load for 50ms periods*/
104          TL0 = 0x00;
105          TR0 = 1;        /*start timer*/
106          IE = 0x82;      /*set interrupts*/
107          timereload = SBUF*1200;/*interval*/
108          timecount = timereload;
109
110          for (;;) PCON = PCON | 0x01; /*idle mode*/
111          }
112       else
113          {
114          for (x=0; x<2048; x++)
115             {
116             sero(adata[x]);   /*output data*/
117             if ((x % 4) != 0) sero(0x2c);  /* comma*/
118             else sero(0x0d);  /*CR*/
119             }
120          }
121       }
```

FIGURE 7–36   C-language data collection program.

and the program returns to await another serial character. If the command received is a time interval for data collection, the main program sets up the sampling and then implements the idle mode. Each time the timer interrupt occurs, the interrupt service routine checks the time and records data if necessary.

Figures 7–35 and 7–36 show the final parts of the programs. Neither of these programs shows anything new or unusual. The formatting routine for the output adds in the commas between the data bytes and a carriage return between the data sets.

Test the System Operationally

The system is tested by running it over several time periods and reviewing the recorded data for accuracy.

7–8   ## SUMMARY

This chapter covers the overall topic of project development. Each of the projects is covered in less detail than the previous one. The reader should be able to fill in the missing details as necessary. Further, the projects are all very minimal in nature; that is, they could all be improved through the addition of one or more features. The data collection system, as an example, could be improved by the addition of a data set counter. Then, when data are transferred, only the newly recorded data are output rather than all 8192 bytes.

The reader now has sufficient knowledge and ability to complete projects using the 8051 family of microcontrollers.

APPENDIX A

Instruction Set Summary

OVERVIEW

Presented below is the complete instruction set for the 8051 microcontroller in summary form.

ARITHMETIC INSTRUCTIONS

ADD	A,Rx	Add the contents of register x to A. Results in A. All flags affected.
ADD	A, direct	Add the contents of direct location to A. Results in A. All flags affected.
ADD	A,@Rx	Add the contents of address from Rx to A. Results in A. All flags affected.
ADD	A,#data	Add #data to A. Results in A. All flags affected.
ADDC	A,Rx	Add the contents of Rx and C to A. Results in A. All flags affected.
ADDC	A,direct	Add the contents of direct location and C to A. Results in A. All flags affected.
ADDC	a,@Rx	Add the contents of address from Rx and C to A. Results in A. All flags affected.
ADDC	A,#data	Add the data and C to A. Results in A. All flags affected.
SUBB	A,Rx	Subtract the contents of Rx and C from A. Results in A. All flags affected.
SUBB	A,direct	Subtract the contents of direct location and C from A. Results in A. All flags affected.
SUBB	A,@Rx	Subtract contents of address given in Rx and C from A. Results in A. All flags affected.
SUBB	A,#data	Subtract data and C from A. Results in A. All flags affected.

INC	A	Increment A. Results in A. No flags are affected.
INC	Rx	Increment contents of Rx. Results in A. No flags are affected.
INC	direct	Increment contents of direct address. Results in direct. No flags are affected.
INC	@Rx	Increment contents of address in Rx. Results in address given in Rx. No flags are affected.
DEC	A	Decrement A. Results in A. No flags are affected.
DEC	Rx	Decrement contents of Rx. Results in Rx. No flags are affected.
DEC	direct	Decrement contents of direct address. Results in direct address. No flags are affected.
DEC	@Rx	Decrement contents of address in Rx. Results in address in Rx. No flags are affected.
INC	DPTR	Decrement 16 bit DPTR. Results in DPTR. No flags are affected.
MUL	AB	Multiply A by B. Results: Low byte in A. High byte in B. OV flag affected, C always cleared.
DIV	AB	Divide A by B. Integer result in A, remainder in B. OV and C flags cleared.
DA	A	Adjust A for BCD addition. Result in A. C flag affected.

LOGICAL OPERATIONS

ANL	A,Rx	AND A with contents of Rx. Results in A. No flags are affected.
ANL	A,direct	AND A with contents of direct address. Results in A. No flags are affected.
ANL	A,@Rx	AND A with contents of address in Rx. Results in A. No flags are affected.
ANL	A,#data	AND A with data. Results in A. No flags are affected.
ANL	direct,A	AND contents of direct address with A. Results in direct address. No flags are affected.
ANL	direct,#data	AND contents of direct address with data. Results in direct address. No flags are affected.
ORL	A,Rx	OR A with contents of Rx. Results in A. No flags are affected.
ORL	A,direct	OR A with contents of direct address. Results in A. No flags are affected.
ORL	A,@Rx	OR A with contents of address in Rx. Results in A. No flags are affected.
ORL	A,#data	OR A with data. Results in A. No flags are affected.
ORL	direct,A	OR contents of direct address with A. Results in direct address. No flags are affected.
ORL	direct,#data	OR contents of direct address with data. Results in direct address. No flags are affected.

XRL	A,Rx	Exclusive OR A with contents of Rx. Results in A. No flags are affected.
XRL	A,direct	Exclusive OR A with contents of direct address. Results in A. No flags are affected.
XRL	A,@Rx	Exclusive OR A with contents of address in Rx. Results in A. No flags are affected.
XRL	direct,A	Exclusive OR contents of direct address with A. Results in direct address. No flags are affected.
XRL	direct,#data	Exclusive OR contents of direct address with data. Results in direct address. No flags affected.
CLR	A	Clear A to zero. A = 0. No flags are affected.
CPL	A	Complement A. Bitwise complement of A. No flags are affected.
RL	A	Rotate A left 1 bit. No flags are affected.
RR	A	Rotate A 1 bit right. No flags are affected.
RLC	A	Rotate A 1 bit left through C. C flag affected.
RRC	A	Rotate A 1 bit right through C. C flag affected.
SWAP	A	Exchange nybbles of A. No flags are affected.

BRANCHING INSTRUCTIONS (FLAGS ARE NOT AFFECTED)

JC	rel	Branch to code address PC+rel if C=1.
JNC	rel	Branch to code address PC+rel if C=0.
JB	bit,rel	Branch to code address PC+rel if contents of bit address is 1.
JNB	bit,rel	Branch to code address PC+rel if contents of bit address are 0.
JBC	bit,rel	Branch to code address PC+rel is contents of bit address =1. Clear contents of bit address.
ACALL	11bit addr	Subroutine call to absolute code address PC(15−11)+11bitaddr. Return address on stack.
LCALL	16bitaddr	Subroutine call to code space at 16bitaddr. Return address on stack.
RET		Return from subroutine. PC loaded from stack.
RETI		Return from interrupt service routine. PC loaded from stack.
AJMP	16bitaddr	Unconditional branch to ,16bitaddr in code space.
LJMP	11bit addr	Unconditional branch to absolute code address PC(15−11)+ 11bitaddr.
SJMP	rel	Unconditional branch to code address PC+rel.
JMP	@A+DPTR	Unconditional branch to code address A+DPTR.
JZ	rel	Branch to code address PC+rel if A=0.
JNZ	rel	Branch to code address PX+rel if A is not equal to 0.
CJNE	A,direct,rel	Branch to code address PC+rel if contents of A are not equal to contents of direct address.

CJNE	A,#data,rel	Branch to code address PC+rel if data are not equal to the contents of A.
CJNE	Rx,#data,rel	Branch to code address PC+rel if contents of Rx are not equal to data.
CJNE	@Rx,#data,rel	Branch to code address PC+rel if contents address in Rx are not equal to data.
DJNZ	Rx,rel	Decrement contents of Rx. Branch to code address PC+rel if new value in Rx is not equal to 0.
DJNZ	direct,rel	Decrement contents of direct address. Branch to code address PC+rel if contents of direct address are not equal to 0.

DATA TRANSFER INSTRUCTIONS

MOV	A,Rx	Copy contents of Rn to A. No flags are affected.
MOV	A,direct	Copy contents of direct address to A. No flags are affected.
MOV	A,@Rx	Copy contents of address in Rx to A. No flags are affected.
MOV	A,#data	Load data into A. No flags are affected.
MOV	Rx,A	Copy contents of A to Rx. No flags are affected.
MOV	Rx,direct	Copy contents of direct address to Rx. No flags are affected.
MOV	Rx,#data	Load data into Rx. No flags are affected.
MOV	direct,A	Copy contents of A to direct address. No flags are affected.
MOV	direct,Rx	Copy contents of Rx to direct address. No flags are affected.
MOV	direct1,direct2	Copy contents of direct2 address to direct1 address. No flags are affected.
MOV	direct,@Rx	Copy contents of address in Rx to direct address. No flags are affected.
MOV	direct,#data	Load data into direct address. No flags are affected.
MOV	@Rx,A	Copy contents of A into address in Rx. No flags are affected.
MOV	@Rx,direct	Copy contents of direct address to address in Rx. No flags are affected.
MOV	@Rx,#data	Load data into address in Rx. No flags are affected.
MOV	DPTR,#16bitdata	Load 16 bit data into DPTR. No flags are affected.
MOVC	A,@A+DPTR	Copy contents of code address A+DPTR to A. No flags are affected.
MOVC	A,@A+PC	Copy contents of code address A+PC to A. No flags are affected.
MOVX	A,@Rx	Copy contents of external data address in Rx to A. No flags are affected.
MOVX	A,@DPTR	Copy contents of external data address in DPTR to A. No flags are affected.
MOVX	@Rx,A	Copy contents of A to external data address in Rx. No flags are affected.
MOVX	@DPTR,A	Copy contents of A to external data address in DPTR. No flags are affected.

PUSH	direct	Copy contents of direct address to next available stack location. No flags are affected.
POP	direct	Copy contents of current stack location to direct address. No flags are affected.
XCH	A,Rx	Exchange contents of A and Rx. No flags are affected.
XCH	A,direct	Exchange contents of A and direct address. No flags are affected.
XCH	A,@Rx	Exchange contents of A and address in Rx. No flags are affected.
XCHD	A,@Rx	Exchange low nybble of A and address in Rx. No flags are affected.

BOOLEAN INSTRUCTIONS

CLR	C	Clear C to zero. C flag is affected.
CLR	bit	Clear bit at bit address. No flags are affected.
SETB	C	Set C to one. C flag is affected.
SETB	bit	Set bit at bit address to one. No flags are affected.
CPL	C	Complement C. C flag is affected.
CPL	bit	Complement bit at bit address. No flags are affected.
ANL	C,bit	AND C with contents of bit address. Results in C. C flag affected.
ANL	C,/bit	AND C with complement of contents of bit address. Results in C. C flag affected.
ORL	C,bit	OR C with contents of bit address. Results in C. C flag affected.
ORL	C,/bit	OR C with complement of contents of bit address. Results in C. C flag affected.
MOV	C,bit	Copy contents of bit address to C. C flag affected.
MOV	bit,C	Copy contents of C to bit address. No flags are affected.

MISCELLANEOUS INSTRUCTIONS

| NOP | | Do absolutely nothing. |

APPENDIX B

ASCII Code Chart

Hex	Character	Hex	Character	Hex	Character	Hex	Character
00	nul	20	sp	40	@	60	`
01	soh	21	!	41	A	61	a
02	stx	22	"	42	B	62	b
03	etx	23	#	43	C	63	c
04	eot	24	$	44	D	64	d
05	enq	25	%	45	E	65	e
06	ack	26	&	46	F	66	f
07	bel	27	'	47	G	67	g
08	bs	28	(	48	H	68	h
09	ht	29	)	49	I	69	i
0A	lf	2A	*	4A	J	6A	j
0B	vt	2B	+	4B	K	6B	k
0C	ff	2C	,	4C	L	6C	l
0D	cr	2D	-	4D	M	6D	m
0E	so	2E	.	4E	N	6E	n
0F	si	2F	/	4F	O	6F	o
10	dle	30	0	50	P	70	p
11	dc1	31	1	51	Q	71	q
12	dc2	32	2	52	R	72	r
13	dc3	33	3	53	S	73	s
14	dc4	34	4	54	T	74	t
15	nak	35	5	55	U	75	u
16	syn	36	6	56	V	76	v
17	etb	37	7	57	W	77	w
18	can	38	8	58	X	78	x
19	em	39	9	59	Y	79	y
1A	sub	3A	:	5A	Z	7A	z
1B	esc	3B	;	5B	[	7B	{
1C	fs	3C	<	5C	\	7C	|
1D	gs	3D	=	5D	]	7D	}
1E	rs	3E	>	5E	^	7E	~
1F	us	3F	?	5F	_	7F	

Index